WALK TO REMEMBER

FIFTEEN SHORTER WALKS IN THE NORTHERN LAKE DISTRICT

Tony Hopkins

The northern Lake District contains some of the finest upland walks in Britain, famous for their views and for the quality of the surrounding countryside. This book includes fifteen of the most interesting shorter routes with comprehensive interpretive notes, offering an insight into the wildlife, agriculture, history and landscape of the area. There are concise route descriptions, maps, photographs and drawings intended to be useful both on the day of the visit and as a momento to bring back pleasant memories. The walks are circular, starting from a convenient parking place and varying in length from three to eight kilometres. The majority are suitable for a wide range of age and fitness, some concentrating on lakesides and valleys, others on steep wooded slopes or fell tops.

Polecat Press

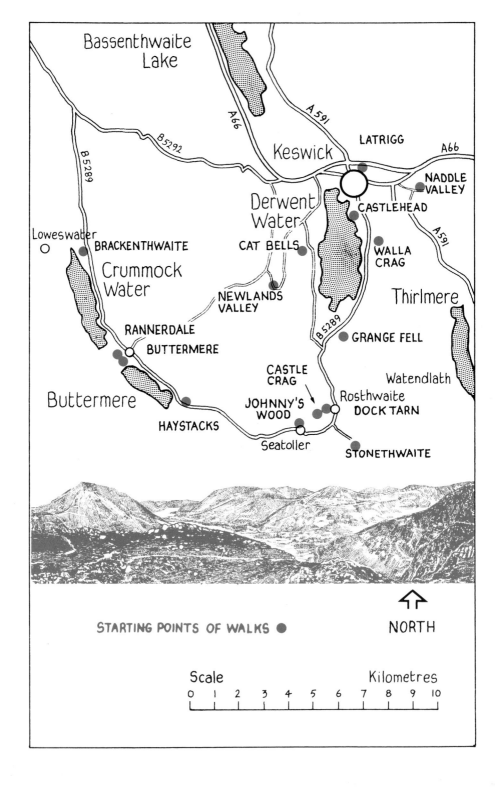

Bassenthwaite
Lake

A66

A591

B5292

Loweswater

B5289

Keswick

LATRIGG

A66

NADDLE
VALLEY

Derwent
Water

CASTLEHEAD

BRACKENTHWAITE

Crummock
Water

CAT BELLS

WALLA
CRAG

A591

NEWLANDS
VALLEY

Thirlmere

RANNERDALE

BUTTERMERE

B5289

GRANGE FELL

Watendlath

Buttermere

CASTLE
CRAG

JOHNNY'S
WOOD

Rosthwaite

DOCK TARN

HAYSTACKS

Seatoller

STONETHWAITE

STARTING POINTS OF WALKS ●

NORTH

Scale   Kilometres
0   1   2   3   4   5   6   7   8   9   10

Contents

Introduction

The unique scenery of the Lake District attracts millions of people every year, but on a brief visit there is little opportunity to discover where the best walks are, or to find answers to the host of questions that come to mind in the course of the day.

This book assembles fifteen of the most attractive and interesting routes in the northern Lake District, the majority requiring little previous walking experience or fitness, selected to illustrate the range of landscapes and habitats that characterise the area.

Selecting a walk

All the walks are circular, starting from places with ample room for parking, but they vary considerably in length, altitude and subject matter. An initial choice of walk may be made by consulting the table below:

	FEATURES				WEATHER			STANDARD		
	Scenery	Wildlife	Geology	Local History	Fog	Rain	Snow (lying)	Level of exertion	Length (in km)	Ascent involved (in m)
1 Latrigg	3	4	2	5	2	3	4	3	8	270
2 Castlehead	3	5	3	4	4	4	4	2	5·5	110
3 Walla Crag	4	4	2	2	1	2	2	3	6·5	300
4 Naddle Valley and Low Rigg	3	4	2	3	3	3	4	3	6	170
5 Cat Bells	4	3	2	3	1	2	1	4	6·5	370
6 Newlands Valley	3	3	3	4	4	3	3	1	6·5	70
7 Castle Crag	4	3	3	3	2	3	2	3	5	200
8 Johnny's Wood	3	4	2	2	3	4	3	2	3·5	150
9 Grange Fell	5	5	4	2	1	1	1	4	7·5	330
10 Dock Tarn and Watendlath	5	5	3	2	1	1	1	4	7·5	390
11 Stonethwaite	3	3	2	2	4	2	4	1	4	50
12 Buttermere	4	3	3	3	4	3	4	1	7	10
13 Hay Stacks	5	3	5	1	1	1	1	5	7·5	480
14 Rannerdale	3	2	3	2	1	2	1	3	6	200
15 Brackenthwaite	3	3	3	3	2	2	3	3	5	150

A wet, misty day on Hay Stacks

A scale of 1 to 5 is used to give some idea of the relative merits of each walk (1 = poor, 2 = fair, 3 = good, 4 = excellent, 5 = outstanding). The same scale is used to indicate the suitability of the routes in bad weather. A low score means that the route is hazardous in those conditions, whilst a high score means it is *comparatively* safe.

An assessment of the overall difficulty of each walk is given on the right (a high score indicating that the walk is strenuous), and on the extreme right is the total length of each walk and the amount of ascent involved.

Timing

No assessment of the duration of each walk is given because this will vary according to fitness, inclination and prevailing weather conditions.

As a general rule allow an hour for every 4 kilometres and add 15 minutes for every 100 metres of ascent; this should allow enough time for a few stops and distractions.

Preparation and safety

Boots or stout shoes are necessary on most of the routes, and a waterproof of some sort (preferably a kagoul) is indispensable. Take warm clothing — the fell tops can be cold even in the summer and conditions can deteriorate quickly. A small rucksack is useful to store items of clothing, bars of chocolate, identification guides . . . and walks books! Always err on the side of safety: consult the local weather forecast, give yourself plenty of time and don't be in too much of a hurry. Be prepared to turn back if conditions deteriorate, and avoid any tempting short cuts, especially on high ground.

Route descriptions

Please note that cairns are piles of stones used as route markers; GR stands for Grid Reference, given to help find the starting point of each walk on Ordnance Survey maps (all walks can be found on the 1 inch: 1 mile Lake District Tourist sheet or the 1 : 25000 North West Lakes Outdoor Leisure map); 'm' and 'km' refer to metres and kilometres. The metric system is used throughout: 1 metre = 1.09 yards, 1 kilometre = 0.62 miles.

5

The maps

A uniform scale of 1 : 25000 has been adopted for maps in the text. All features described in the body of the text are incorporated, and any walls and buildings of use in route-finding have been retained. Contours are in metres, north is always towards the top of the page, and the walking route is superimposed in a second colour with its starting point clearly indicated.

On the walk

Paths in the Lake District are heavily used and it is in everyone's interest to follow the Country Code. In particular, fasten all gates, keep to the recognised path, and take any litter home. Most of the routes follow recognised footpaths but there are several cases where no right of way exists and the path is by permission of the landowner. Please be particularly considerate when passing farmhouses or crossing agricultural land, leave machinery and livestock alone and, if you wish to take a dog, keep it under control on a lead.

The routes may change from time to time according to agreements between the National Park Authority, who administer the footpaths system, and the farmer. Stiles and gates may be changed too, so common sense should be employed when walking a footpath, no matter what a published guide may say.

Most of the Lake District lies within the boundary of the National Park; this accounts for an area of over 224,000 hectares, for which special conservation safeguards exist and provision for visitors is made. Wardens and Information Centres offer advice to walkers and officers liaise with landowners over land management and rights of way. The National Trust is strongly represented too, owning over 50,000 hectares and participating in management agreements to preserve both the landscape and the way of life. Thus the scenery described in this book is the product of many years of endeavour and is part of a national heritage, to be valued and enjoyed by everyone.

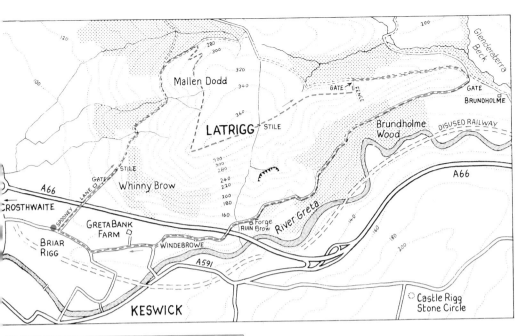

Walk One
LATRIGG

SPOONEY LANE — LATRIGG — BRUNDHOLME — WINDEBROWE; 8km

Latrigg has always been a favourite walk for the people of Keswick, offering a unique view over the town towards Derwent Water and Borrowdale, but it also provides one of the easiest routes to any worthwhile summit, with a gradual incline and a great deal of associated wildlife and history.

Start at GR 267242. Park on the Briar Rigg road opposite a sideroad to a small housing estate.Take the wide track leading north, signposted 'public bridleway to Skiddaw'. This is Spooney Lane.

The hedgerow alongside the main road is neatly maintained, reflecting a sense of harmony and order. Around the corner in Spooney Lane the situation is different, the hedge having at one time been allowed to grow rampant, too tall, too 'gappy' and too difficult to re-lay. The result has been the introduction of a wire fence with only fragments of the old hedge left to tell the tale. To appreciate the role that hedges once played in the area it is better to be on Latrigg with a view to Bassenthwaite, but a little further along Spooney Lane, just before the bridge, the section to the right at least offers a clue to its pedigree.

Within the space of a few metres there are bushes or trees of holly, ash, elder, hawthorn, sycamore, oak, dog rose, and beech. The diversity suggests that the hedge is very old, probably of medieval origin, and since it was planted on both sides of the track we can assume that Spooney Lane has been there for at least as long. The way back, past Windebrowe and Greta Bank Farm, will provide a few more clues . . . .

7

If it is spring there will be violets and Jack-by-the-hedge in flower, otherwise cow parsley, crosswort and woundwort will cover the verge.

Go over the bridge and up the track.

Before the A66 was built the field on the left stretched right back to Briar Rigg Road. According to the 1840 Tithe Map it was called Spoonah Close; the area ahead was Spoonah Green and the field to the right was called Groat Field. The groat (a silver coin worth 4d, i.e. 4 old pennies) went out of circulation in 1662, and the name perhaps refers to the relative size or quality of the field.

Continue past a building on the left, and through a wicket gate to the right of a five-bar gate. Continue up the track.

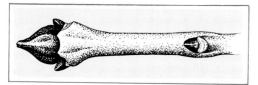

Ash twig

The track, which seems remarkably robust for such an underused route, was constructed around 1800 to allow farm machinery to get up onto the slopes of Latrigg.

The marshy ground to the right contains meadowsweet and yellow loosestrife, whilst the drier banks are inhabited by bramble and the inevitable foxglove. The wooded slope to the right is called Whinny Brow, and since 'whin' is Old Norse for gorse it would seem that gorse bushes have always been a feature of Latrigg.

The fenced area contains ash and larch trees, but close to the track there are several fine thickets of gorse, bursting with yellow flowers in early summer and producing a heavy coconut-scented fug which attracts bees. The foliage of gorse was once used as kindling wood and to fuel bakers' ovens; its capacity to burn fiercely makes it a notorious fire risk in an age of cigarette ends.

Go over the stile to the side of a gate and continue uphill, still keeping to the track which leads alongside a mature spruce plantation before reaching an 'S'-bend and a small stream or gill. At the fork just beyond the bend keep left with the plantation still to your left. Continue past the plantation and over another small bridge. The track bears left and begins to level out.

There is an excellent view to the left; Skiddaw dominates the north whilst to the north-west is Bassenthwaite Lake. The level ground between Bassenthwaite and Derwent Water attracted the first Neolithic farmers to settle in the Lake District and the rich alluvial soil has been intensively used ever since, either for pasture, corn or root crops. Turnip-growing was an especially important development in the area because it revolutionised the winter feeding of sheep, but like most innovations the turnip took a while to catch on; it was not until 1793 when a Mr Atkinson 'was the first in the fruitful and beautiful vale of Bassen-thwaite that ventured to sow so much as four acres of turnips in a year; and it being in his younger days, he was sneeringly laughed at by his neighbours'. This observation was penned by William Dickinson in 1850, by which date turnips were an accepted winter fodder, though sheep were also given pine branches to nibble in the belief that the resin acted beneficially on the system of animals confined to such a watery diet . . . .

Just beyond the A66/A591 roundabout is Crosthwaite, its church visible beyond a school field. The church is dedicated to St Kentigern who arrived here about 553 whilst on his way from Glasgow to Wales. Apparently he was fleeing for his life, but when he heard about the people of the mountains who worshipped false gods he stopped off long enough to erect a cross in a clearing, hence the name Crosthwaite.

In more recent times the name Hardwicke Drummond Rawnsley figures prominently in local and national affairs. He was vicar of Crosthwaite at the turn of the century but is best remembered as co-founder of the National Trust. What is sometimes forgotten is that he was also a great activist and led several important campaigns to open the fells to walkers. Two thousand people took part in a mass trespass along this path after the route to Latrigg had been blocked. This was in the late 1880s, long before access to the countryside had become a national issue.

Continue along the track to the right of another spruce plantation until a grassy path leads three-quarters right up the hillside.

Opposite the path is a small group of hawthorns, looking rather out of place among the conifers. The flowers, produced during the early summer, are prolific but short-lived and the old name of May blossom, referring to the appearance of the flowers on May Day, was made nonsense by the change from the Julian to the Gregorian calendar in 1752.

Walk up the steep grassy track, which zig-zags several times before heading around the slope of Mallen Dodd.

Bracken clothes the ground but it is not very dense, allowing other plants to survive so long as they can also tolerate being grazed heavily by Swaledale sheep. The bushy grey lichen is called *Cladonia*; in Scandinavia a closely-related species is the staple food for reindeer.

The River Greta with Latrigg in the distance

The path turns abruptly to the left on the top of Latrigg. Before following this path walk over to the right for an excellent view southwards.

Like many towns with a crowded history, Keswick seems a disorganised jumble of streets and houses, surrounded in this case by a cordon of green fields which enhance the beauty of the lakeside.

To the east of Derwent Water are Walla Crag and Bleaberry Fell, on the south shore is Borrowdale, guarded by King's How and Castle Crag, and to the west is the fine range of fells capped by Crag Hill and Grizedale Pike.

Now follow the path again which makes its way north-east with the hilltop to your left and a steep slope to your right. Continue along the cairned path to an old drystone wall (topped by a fence) with a stile in it. Go through the stile keeping to the same line on the other side.

Walls can be old too and this one bears several signs of antiquity, not least the amount of moss and lichen growing on it. The hilltop has no bracken at all, probably because the soil is too thin and exposed

and spring frosts kill the young fronds. Heather and bilberry would grow here if it were not for the sheep. As it is the only place to find bilberry is in the crevices of the wall, and the ground cover is mostly fescue grass.

Moles are quite common here though their hills are not always obvious. Each mole excavates its own tunnel system and produces several hills in the process, but once it has finished the digging its whole life revolves around waiting for worms to drop in for a meal.

A mole has an active hunting period of about four hours followed by a similar period of rest, so that it gets through four 'days' to our one. For centuries farmers have been trying to eradicate moles ('mow-diwarps') from their land, and in this area they were once successful. According to a report submitted to the Board of Agriculture in 1797 their inspectors 'scarce ever saw a mole-hill upon the enclosed grounds of most parts of Cumberland', and they attributed this to the letting of the mole-catching, any fee being raised by local parishes. There are now a lot more of the creatures about, on in-bye and intake as well as on fells and commons, and the skilled job of catching them is a dying art. The latest form of pest control is to put worms laced with strychnine into the tunnels and trust to the moles' gluttony.

Keep to the path. After a little way there is a wood to your left. Walk parallel with this, still on the path, until you reach a fence (with old hawthorns). At this turn left, then right through a gate. Continue along the rutted track with the wood to your left. When the wood ends follow the crest of the ridge eastwards.

View from Latrigg summit — south clockwise to north

This is an ancient 'green way' known as Wigton Road. To the right the A66 spoils what would otherwise be an attractive view of the wooded banks of the River Greta ('Greta' is Old Norse for rocky stream), the Naddle Valley and St John's Vale beyond.

Ahead and to the left, the lower slopes of Skiddaw and Blencathra are separated by Glenderaterra Beck, with Lonscale Fell to the west and Blease Fell to the east.

The 'in-bye' farmland beyond Lonscale Farm comes to an abrupt end as the ground rises steeply. Beyond the last wall the vegetation is dominated by bracken and rushes and the quality of grazing is drastically reduced. This is the sort of country favoured by foxes, though these days they are of the red lowland type rather than the large grey-coloured variety hunted by John Peel in the early 19th century. Peel was born and raised at Caldbeck, over 15km to the north of here across the wilds of Skiddaw Forest, but it was nothing for him to cover that distance on foot with his 14 couple of hounds, and hunts of 110 - 130km were not unknown at about that time. Today there is still a Blencathra pack of hounds, kennelled at Threlkeld, and although the huntsmen still go on foot the foxes do not seem to be as energetic as they once were.

The path leads down to a gate. Turn right down the metalled road and follow it down to Brundholme Wood. There is an alternative path which bears off the road to the left; this offers a pleasant woodland/river-side walk but is not recommended if you are short of time or are tired. Instead, keep to the road.

At this point the woodland is mostly birch, and since its seeds need light to germinate

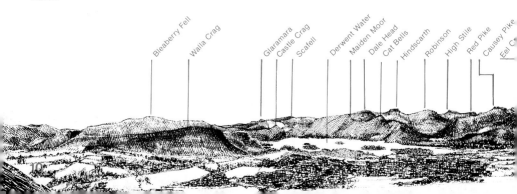

Bleaberry Fell Walla Crag Glaramara Castle Crag Scafell Derwent Water Maiden Moor Dale Head Cat Bells Hindscarth Robinson High Stile Red Pike Causey Pike Eel C

this is a sign that the original oaks were block-felled. Birch is often called 'the lady of the woods' because it is slim and graceful, but it is worthless as a timber crop and is considered a weed by foresters. There are other trees here however, including oak, sycamore and wych elm, with an understorey of hazel. A good mixed habitat which birds favour because it offers a variety of food and shelter.

Continue along the road for several hundred metres.

There are some very fine banks of foxgloves to the right, flowering profusely in most years. Once the flowers have died the seedheads make good table decorations, but make sure that all the seeds have gone if you are tempted to take any home. This is not just in the name of conservation but also to avoid a host of unwanted seedlings appearing in your garden. One of the nastiest of all alien plants, the giant hogweed, is thought to be dispersed not only by wind and water, but also by amateur flower-arrangers in search of something dramatic.

The road eventually leads out of the wood, with a small stone ruin to the left.

The area to the left is Forge Brow, a name dating back to the 16th century when this hillside overlooked the smelting furnaces at Brigham - 'the finest works of their kind in Europe', producing copper ingots for Elizabeth I.

Cross the A66 and bear right along the road.

The noise from the traffic can be irritating, but we have learned to live with progress in a way that would have appalled past generations. The first turnpike road reached Keswick in 1761, at first to unanimous celebration, but second thoughts soon gave way to deep misgivings by those affluent enough to have finer feelings about the environment. Residents like Wordsworth and Canon Rawnsley fought bitterly and with some success to keep railways out of the main valleys. But the ironworks of industrial Cumberland needed coke and a Penrith to Cockermouth Railway was duly constructed in 1865. The line passed through Keswick, just the other side of the river from here, and it brought the first real wave of tourism.

To walkers on the slopes of Latrigg the railway would only have been an occasional distraction. As Bradley wrote in 1901, 'At long intervals there is a rattle and brief commotion, a cloud of smoke, a stampede of wood pigeons, and a scuttle or rabbits, and the horrid thing is gone'.

Keep to the road, which continues straight ahead, past Windebrowe.

Windebrowe appears on the parish record of 1594. 'Old Windebrowe', the collection of buildings on the roadside, once housed a stables and is still used as such, by the Calvert Trust's adventure centre for the disabled which opened in 1978. Rainsley Calvert, who died in 1795 at the age of 21, was a close friend and supporter of Wordsworth, and it was his legacy of £900 which gave the poet freedom to become a full-time writer. Rainsley's older brother, William, lent the house to William and Dorothy Wordsworth who lived here for most of 1794 (during which the *Windy Brow Notebook,* including such poems as 'Salisbury Plain', was written).

A few metres along the road is the entrance

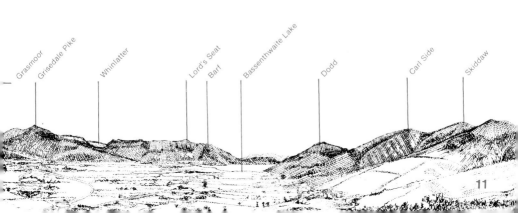

Grasmoor Grisedale Pike Whinlatter Lord's Seat Barf Bassenthwaite Lake Dodd Carl Side Skiddaw

11

to Windebrowe, a 'mansion with shrub-
beries', listed as 'Greta Bank' on most old
maps but renamed about 1920. A little
further on are some fine old trees, the
remnants of what must have been a
majestic avenue. On the left as the road
bears left is a superb oak, probably a
pollard, its trunk slightly spiralled (perhaps
it was twinned, two saplings together). Its
top must have been lopped when still a
young tree and the resulting set of shoots
allowed to grow into sturdy ascending
boughs.

Across the road at this point is a horse
chestnut. Behind it is another oak, situated
outside a small wood (actually an old
orchard). Compare this oak with the one on
the left of the road and it will be obvious
that it was not interfered with in the same
way. Now compare it with yet another
mature oak standing out in the middle of
the field. Obviously oaks can grow into
different shapes; the one on the right close
to the horse chestnut grew on the edge of,
or just inside the wood, developing into a
tall tree with few heavy side branches,
whilst the one out in the field has always
had light around it and has developed a
semi-circular crown. Neither of these trees
has moved but the wood edge has been
pushed back, to confuse both the trees and
local historians..

**Continue about 50m along the track, where
the road bears right.**

Dog's mercury

Few trees are given individual names, but
where they are it is usually with good
reason; the oak to the left (where a track
leads down to the river) is called the Hang-
man's Tree, its precise history obscure but
probably tragic. The triple-stemmed oak in
the field to the right bears a name too, the
General's Tree, this time following a less
sinister episode in the estate's history. In
the 1930s Brigadier-General Spedding
decided to improve the quality of his sheep
stock by introducing a Border-Leicester
ram. The ram (or 'tupp'), called John
Wooley, was not of benign disposition and
its owner was obliged on one memorable
occasion to seek refuge in this tree. The
experiment with Border-Leicesters was not
continued.

**Bear right, keeping to the road as it passes
Greta Bank Farm and continues west to a
junction.**

Putting a few of the clues together it is now
obvious that the hedge on the right, hiding
a row of oak stumps, was part of the original estate and has outlived more imposing
structures, buildings and trees, that may
have stood close-by. Woodland plants like
dog's mercury, growing along the verge,
suggest that the hedge began its career
even before Kentigern, not as an enclosure
perhaps, but certainly as a fragment of
woodland left after the first forest clearance.

Turn right, back to Spooney Lane.

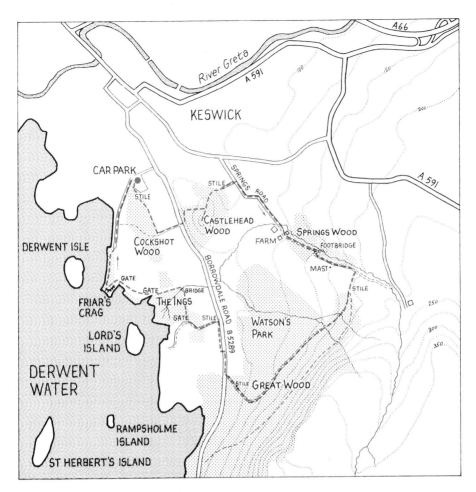

Walk Two
CASTLEHEAD

**COCKSHOT — GREAT WOOD —
FRIAR'S CRAG; 5.5km**

A gentle walk linking five ancient woods and incorporating meadow, pasture, lakeside and a splendid view of Borrowdale. In spite of the route's proximity to Keswick and the tourist honeypot of the north-east shore, most people find it disarmingly enjoyable. It is not wild or remote, simply beautiful.

Start at GR 266229, on the lakeside car park just north of Cockshot Wood.

The grounds of the car park are worth a few minutes inspection because of the wide assortment of trees that have been planted, including whitebeam, cherry, field maple, beech, ash, oak and willow. During the early summer the grassy banks are interesting too, bugle, lady's mantle and pignut combining in an unusual association of woodland and meadow plants. Pignut, a delicate little 'umbellifer' rather like dwarf cow parsley, used to be sought after by country children who lived in blissful ignorance of the fact that a 17th century herbalist had recommended it for its aphrodisiac or 'venery' properties. The 'nut' is in fact difficult to locate without excavating an unsightly hole.

Make for the south corner of the car park, entering Cockshot Wood via a stile. Turn left and walk south along the wood edge.

This is not an especially imposing wood (wait until you see Castlehead); its oak and ash trees have been augmented by beech and sycamore, both introduced by man. Sycamore in particular is cordially hated by naturalists, which may seem odd considering it is a hardwood tree and hardwoods are what naturalists are trying to conserve. Sycamore's flaw is in its pedigree as a native tree; it has only been here for about 400 years and did not arrive by fair means. Oak, ash and most of the others got to Britain by spreading sedately westward over Europe as the ice retreated and the climate improved. About 5,500 years ago the English Channel severed the land-bridge and many plants and animals arrived at the French and Belgian coasts too late. Thus our native British flora is what got here before the deluge, and it took many centuries for man to provide some logical additions. Unfortunately all the associated insects and birds of the European forests could not be so easily transported, resulting in some very dull and lifeless woods.

Continue along the path for about 300m.

Cockshot got its name from Cock-shut i.e. twilight. It is a mixed wood and has a good proportion of oak with hazel growing as an understorey. Vernal flowers like wood anemone and dog's mercury make up the herb layer.

At the cross-roads of paths turn left, out of the wood and up a path with a hedge alongside it.

Some plants seem to like growing in the shade of hedges, the prime example being Jack-by-the-hedge or hedge garlic, which grows here during early summer. The leaves are large and rounded and taste mildly of garlic (unlike ramsons, which despite what some books say is capable of fumigating every brain cell at the first bite). The flower spike is tall and when the little white flowers have fallen they leave thin green seed-pods. Look closely and you may find a tiny orange egg attached to one of the pods, laid by an orange-tip butterfly. The caterpillar feeds quite openly on the developing pods but is still well camouflaged, thin and green and probably smelling of garlic.

Over the hedge to the left is an attractive view of meadowland and pasture, with Skiddaw brooding in the distance.

The path leads onto the Borrowdale road. Cross the road and turn left towards the northern edge of the wood, then bear right uphill.

You are now among some of the finest trees in the Lake District, oaks of great character and distinction. It is heartening to see that there are also many young oaks too, presumably because Castlehead is not grazed by sheep which would nibble any seedlings to death. Regeneration of native woodland is a national problem largely caused by abuse and thoughtlessness.

Where the path levels out and the fence to the left meets the corner of a field, turn right, a detour which takes you to the top of Castlehead.

The view is remarkably good, especially to the south, of Derwent Water and its delta flanked by a dense skirt of trees and overlooked by open fells and peaks. A busy landscape, almost too full to bear analysis. Instead look at the rock on which you are standing, a fine-grained and very hard material called dolerite bearing tiny crystals of augite. In fact you are possibly standing on a volcano, for dolerite is an igneous rock forced in a molten state through the earth's crust several million years ago. That it does not resemble a volcano today is the result of weathering, in particular by the boulder-filled glaciers which have sandpapered away the surface.

Retrace your route back to the field corner on the wood edge and back onto the path. Continue north-east, downhill.

The footpath through Castlehead Wood, shaded by a mature ▷
oak

Bird song is a characteristic of these woods though it is often difficult to separate the sounds and identify the culprits. During May and June the trio of leaf warblers are particularly in evidence. The most memorable of these is the wood warbler which produces a jingle something like 'stip-stip-stititititipswee'. If this sounds complicated then remember it as a single note that gains speed and ends as a trill. The willow warbler is responsible for another distinctive song, this time a descending ripple, which transcribes onto paper as 'se-se-se-se-see-su-su-suit-suit-sueet-sueetew'. Not surprisingly most people find it impossible to imagine this sort of jibberish as a lovely wistful bird song. The last of the trio presents no difficulty however, for the chiffchaff just goes 'chiff chaff'.

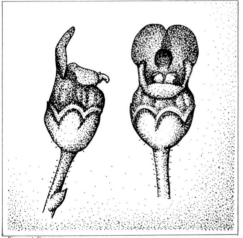
Figwort flowers

The path bears left and out of the wood via a stile. Continue along the tarmac track to a road, at which turn right, heading south-east.

This is Springs Road, a smart suburb of Keswick with some immaculate front gardens full of azalias and laburnums. There is a good view back to Castlehead which stands aloof but contained within the patchwork of meadows.

Continue along the road, which ends in a farmyard. Follow the footpath signs, over the bridge and between the farm buildings into Springs Wood.

This is a fine example of a coppice, the trees once managed for under-wood rather than timber, i.e. for poles which could then be used for basket making, fencing or for the local pencil-making industry in Keswick. Coppice woodland once covered much of England but over the past fifty years it has almost disappeared. Old people are often accused of looking back on their youth through rose-tinted glasses, but in the case of romantic walks along flower-covered woodland rides they are perfectly correct. There really were more flowers in the old days when the coppiced hazels allowed in plenty of spring sunshine, and primroses, bluebells and anemones produced dazzling mosaics of colour.

Walk uphill with the stream on your left, until just before a footbridge. Bear right along a broad track, which then bears left, along the edge of a wood.

This small wood is called 'North Willy Howe Planting' on the 1840 Tithe Map. The trees are mostly downy birch, with some rowan and sycamore. In the early summer the open canopy allows a carpet of bluebells and stitchwort to brighten the banks.

Continue past a radio mast until a path leads right, towards Great Wood. Follow this path, a wall to your left, and enter the wood via a stile. Walk downhill for a few metres until just after a small stream, when a large vehicle track can be seen through a clearing in the larch trees to the right. Bear right along a minor path to join this track and follow it downhill.

Today Great Wood and Watson's Park (to the right) are composed essentially of larch. They present a useful contrast with Castlehead, and bear witness to how native woodland can be sacrificed to profit or popular notions of beauty. Larch is one of the trees that never made it across the land bridge and had to be introduced (from the Alps) in the 18th century, not for its timber but as an ornamental tree to grace country estates.

Walk downhill along the track for several hundred metres (ignoring any side paths) until it meets a gate. Go over the stile next to this gate and bear right to the

Borrowdale road, at which turn right. Walk along the roadside for about 100m then go through a stile on the left and bear right through a small wood to a gravel drive. Turn left and after about 75m go through a wicket gate to the right and into another wood.

This is The Ings, an example of alder and willow 'carr' (marshy woodland) with a profusion of meadowsweet, yellow flag and marsh marigold. There is also figwort, a tall plant with a square stem and tiny round purple/red flowers, much frequented by wasps. The leaves are often eaten-away until they resemble green lace; the creature responsible for this is the grub of a little weevil called *Cionus*. Most weevils are boring little things (literally — they bore through leaves and seeds) but the adult *Cionus* is very attractive and can be found sitting on the seed-heads, but *very* well camouflaged!

Go over a footbridge and bear left until another wicket gate leads you onto parkland on the lake shore.

The east shore of Derwent Water, looking south

Derwent Water now becomes the abiding influence, and Lord's Island, to the south, attracts immediate attention. It is steeped in history, most notably because of its association with the unfortunate Radcliffe family.

Sir Francis Radcliffe fled to the island after being driven out of Northumberland by Parliamentary forces, but his manor house on Lord's Island turned out to be an insecure retreat and was destroyed in 1640.

In 1715 his descendant James Radcliffe, third and last Earl of Derwentwater, exhibited the same fatal family trait of being on the losing side, this time taking up the Jacobite cause. He was imprisoned in the Tower of London and would have been spared had he acknowledged George I and the Protestant religion, but he remained loyal to his cousin James Stuart and he was beheaded on February 24th, 1716 at the age of 27. Bright red lights were seen in the sky, the first recorded appearance of the aurora borealis or northern lights, which were referred to thereafter as Lord Derwentwater's Lights.

An obvious path bears right over two small footbridges, leading to a wooded knoll just after a small bay.

This view of Friar's Crag and Derwent Water may give you an uneasy sensation of déjà vu. In fact, it has appeared on so many chocolate boxes and calendars that its image is probably imprinted on half the subconscious minds in Britain. Even the great Victorian traveller John Ruskin considered it 'one of the three or four most beautiful views in Europe'. His opinion was tempered by nostalgia, however, for as a child his first memory was of being taken by his nurse to the brow of the crag where 'the intense joy, mingled with awe, that I had in looking through the mossy roots, over the crag, into the dark lake, has associated itself more or less with all twining roots of trees ever since'.

Like Castlehead, Friar's Crag is made of dolerite, similar in composition to the basalt of Fingals Cave or the Giant's Causeway.

Go through the wicket gate, left and up around the point of Friar's Crag. From there walk north along the lakeside to join a metalled road.

The island close-by to the west is Derwent Isle (sometimes called Vicar's Isle) which is the largest of the Derwent Water group and was once a little enclave for the families of German miners, working the nearby lead and copper mines in the 16th and 17th centuries. It is recorded in the Crosthwaite parish register that in the twenty years after 1565 a total of 176 christenings took place involving German fathers, and one of the descendants of those families, Sir John Rawlinson, became Mayor of London.

Continue north along the road.

To the left are jetties and landing stages offering steam-boat trips over the lake.

The car park is a little further on, to the right.

The Ings in spring; an alder wood carpeted by marsh plants

18

Walk Three
WALLA CRAG

GREAT WOOD — ASHNESS BRIDGE — WALLA CRAG — RAKEFOOT; 6.5km

Walla Crag is one of the best-loved of the lower Lakeland Fells, its panorama quite breathtaking and well worth the modest climb involved. The walk also offers woodland, bracken-covered slopes beneath precipitous crags, high moorland and a fine view over Derwent Water.

Start at GR 272213. Park in Great Wood car park, 2.5km south-west of Keswick, just above the Borrowdale road. Leave the car park by a stile next to a gate, on the south-east side of the parking area. The path curves quickly up and right, to a signed junction. Follow the southern route, way-marked 'Ashness Bridge'.

This part of Great Wood makes you wonder how the place got its name (on the Tithe Map it is called Waterage Bank Wood), but it was once a tract of majestic oaks, a wilderness held in awe and rarely entered.

Fragments of the original wood still survive, but as islands amid more recent conifer planting. Above the path to the left are larches, not without their own beauty especially when, as in this case, there are also rowans and ash trees to break the uniformity.

To the right is an area of coppiced hazel and small saplings, too young as yet to obscure the view of Cat Bells and Causey Pike on the other side of Derwent Water.

Continue to a small footbridge.

The little stream is called Cat Gill, described in 1759 as still being a likely stronghold of wild cats, 'the most fierce and daring animals we have'. The report, by Clarke, goes on to observe that they 'seem to be of the tyger kind', and that twelve were killed during Whitsun week not far away. Not surprisingly the wild cat became extinct in England by the early 19th century.

A reduction in the level of keepering in the Scottish Highlands this century has resulted in a rapid extension towards the Border, so perhaps wild cats will recolonise Cumbria before too long and return to former haunts. If they did it would probably be some time before anybody realised it; wild cats are very shy, not daring or fierce, and certainly not inclined to brush around people's ankles.

The damp face of the rock to the left of the stream is overhung with honeysuckle, the flowers of which have an indescribably beautiful scent. In shadowy conditions the plant produces no flowers however, and its old name of woodbine is more appropriate. The folk ballad 'Spencer the Rover' is just one of many traditional stories referring to the plant:

'With the night fast approaching, to the woods he resorted, with woodbine and ivy his bed for to make.'

Holly and ivy grow here also, linked by their choice of soil and a thread of pre-Christian history. They are endowed with magical power, the holly male and the ivy female, proof against evil and an important part of the mid-winter festival.

Ivy

Go over the footbridge; the path descends with a wall to your right.

On the other side of the wall is one of the better remnants of Great Wood, some sturdy oaks clothed in lichens and looking good for another century.

leader climbs up trailing the rope behind him, which he clips into small metal 'nuts' that he places in crevices in the rock, whilst the second holds the end of the rope firmly. Should the leader slip, the second holds the rope and the metal nuts act as pulleys, stopping the leader falling all the way

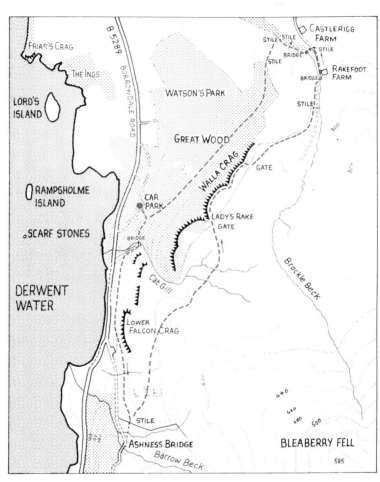

After a few metres the path bears left leading onto a more open hillside with high crags to the left.

This is Falcon Crag - named after the peregrine falcons which still haunt the general area. Look at Lower Falcon Crag and you are likely to see climbers spreadeagled on the 53 metre-high rock-face, for this is a popular climbing route. In each climbing party there is a leader and a second; the

down. The second climber follows with the comparative safety of a rope from above.

Natural history and climbing are often thought to be incompatible (especially when climbers indulge in 'gardening' to clear vegetation from clefts and ledges), but birds of prey like the peregrine have had to learn to co-exist, to cope with a certain level of disturbance.

After passing the second buttress (Lower Falcon Crag) the path rises gently and splits; go straight on, along the path way-marked 'Ashness Bridge'.

There is a good viewpoint to the right of the sign. The 'Jaws of Borrowdale' to the south-west are impressively toothed, but the most remarkable feature is how heavily wooded they seem. This is partly an illusion, the major woods stacked in a line to mask fellsides and fields, but there is no doubt that there really is a high density of tree cover, most of it hardwood timber. The exaggerated slopes and compressed perspective lend the view a flavour of J.R.R. Tolkein, the road to Rivendell.

The path rises gradually via a short series of steps, then crosses a narrow stream.

Usually a quiet tinkling little gill, but storms turn it into a torrent of flying boulders. To the left, uphill, is a low evergreen shrub, a juniper, bearing small dark berries which take two or three years to ripen. Crush a few spiky leaves and they will give off a strong refreshing smell just like gin, the product of volatile oils called monoter-penes. Juniper has a reputation as an aphrodisiac, or as a 'resister of Pestilence', but it can be poisonous and should be treated with respect. It is, incidentally, the favourite foodplant of the elk.

Continue to a ladder stile over a wall.

If you have the time and inclination, go over the stile and walk to Ashness Bridge, about 250m away. Just upstream from the bridge the stones are worn smooth by countless photographers cuffing their boots or elbows trying to frame the perfect pic-ture. It is one of the most photographed scenes in Britain, Derwent Water and Skiddaw in the background and the little packhorse bridge in the foreground. Walk back to the ladder stile and cross it.

A few metres from the wall turn obliquely uphill; the path is sometimes rocky but usually clear on the ground.

There are one or two more juniper bushes, neatly clipped by sheep but still looking healthy. Juniper has one of the best pedigrees of any Lakeland tree, having arrived shortly after the Ice Age when the

climate and soil would not support other species.

The view north of Derwent Water is dominated by the islands, particularly St Herbert's Island to the left and Rampsholme to the right. Between them lies a tiny scattering of rocks called Scarf Stones, actually lying due south of Ramps-holme. This is a favourite loafing place for waterbirds, especially cormorants, who are shy of people and are often subject to unofficial 'control' because of their efficiency at catching fish.

Eventually the path levels out and becomes grassy.

There are several marshy places, worth inspecting because they contain interesting plants such as cross-leaved heath and butterwort. The latter species was known as rot-grass because it was supposed to cause foot-rot in sheep, but it got its more usual name because it was thought to protect the dairy from fairies. The leaves are pale green with curled edges, bluntly pointed, with a slightly slippery surface designed to catch flies and thereby provide the plant with essential nutrients.

Continue along the wide path, heading north-east.

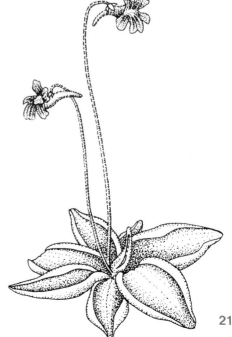

Butterwort

21

To the right there is a fascinating patchwork of vegetation: heather, bracken and mat-grass. Surprisingly sheep find mat-grass, *Nardus stricta*, virtually inedible and it usually grows in the most impoverished conditions, often on the sites of ancient clearings. In the winter it turns white, contrasting with the brown bracken and black heather.

The view to the south-east unfolds gradually, a fine sweep of heather moorland rising to Bleaberry Fell. Heather is the food-plant of some of the most dramatic upland insects such as the northern eggar and emperor moths, both of which have day-flying males who career erratically over the moor at break-neck speed trying to find females. They can detect a potential mate at a range of several hundred metres, a feat made possible by incredibly sensitive feathered antennae capable of registering a few molecules of scent. The emperor is on the wing in April and May, the northern eggar in May and June.

The path bears right, contouring around a headstream of Cat Gill.

There is a good view to the left, over Derwent Water; directly opposite is a green corridor to the Newlands valley, framed between Cat Bells to the left and the forested knoll of Swinside to the right. Behind Newlands can be seen Barrow and Causey Pike, with Hopegill Head and Crag Hill in the distance.

To the north-west is Bassenthwaite Lake, owned by the National Park Authority and one of the least accessible of waters. The more people encouraged to enjoy the countryside the less attractive it can become, and this is particularly true for the wildlife associated with lakes. It seems only right that there should be a few quiet places where access is partly restricted.

Continue north-east then north, to a wicket gate.

Heather moorland is still the major feature to the right, most attractive in late August when the flowers cast a mauve or purple wash over the whole landscape. At other times these are 'black lands', and Bleaberry Fell, rising to 585m (1,932ft) can be rather dour and foreboding. Bilberries (bleaberries) are rather a scarce crop because the bushes are heavily grazed by sheep, but a search of the less accessible banks and crags may produce enough of the blue-black berries in July to make a pie, a gastronomic marvel with a transatlantic reputation.

Go through the wicket gate.

The gap to the left, the deep scar on Walla Crag visible from miles around, is Lady's Rake. This was supposed to be the escape route taken by Lady Radcliffe in the 17th century, fleeing with the family treasure from Parliamentary forces who were attack-

View from Walla Crag summit — south-west clockwise to north

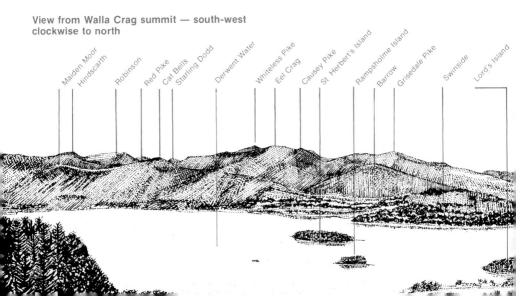

Maiden Moor · Hindscarth · Robinson · Red Pike · Cat Bells · Starling Dodd · Derwent Water · Whiteless Pike · Eel Crag · Causey Pike · St. Herbert's Island · Rampsholme Island · Barrow · Grisedale Pike · Swinside · Lord's Island

Mat-grass, bracken and heather; Bleaberry Fell in the distance

ing Lord's Island. Why she chose such a tortuous route is a mystery; gold coins found among the boulders in subsequent years offer convenient corroboration.

Continue to the summit.

A mighty view, worthy of a much more exhausting climb! The distant peaks are impressive, but so too are the woods and fields in the foreground: Watson's Park, mostly larch trees, then a gap to a narrow ribbon of woodland screening a white house, then another gap to the domed oakwood of Castlehead. To the left, on the lakeshore, lies The Ings, with Friar's Crag to the left and Cockshot Wood (with its large car park) a little way beyond.

To the left of Keswick look for Crosthwaite Church, in line with the lower slope of Thornthwaite Forest on the eastern shore of Bassenthwaite Lake. This was the pivot about which civilisation flourished during the Dark Ages, and is of more recent literary interest as the resting place of Robert Southey, a Poet Laureate little remembered by posterity.

From the summit cairn walk along the path parallel with the crag face.

The trees on the summit of Walla Crag are mostly birch with a few rowan, having grown up after a disastrous fire in 1925 which removed most of the existing cover.

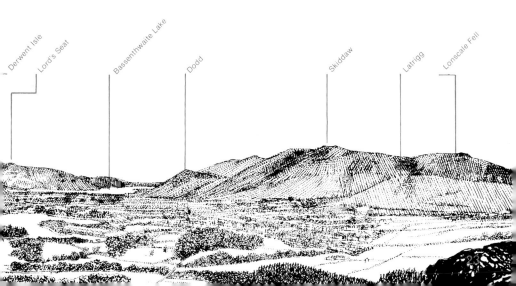

The parallel path leads to a wicket gate through a wall. Walk along the wide grassy path to rejoin the wall, then continue alongside this and downhill, bearing left to cross a stile alongside a gate.

The gateposts are slate slabs, traditional in the Lake District and much more hard-wearing than they look. To the right is the Brockle Beck (Brock = badger of course!), an attractive stream drawing its water from peat-capped fells, and therefore nutrient-poor and acidic in nature. The banks of the beck are wooded with ash, rowan and birch, but there is a scrubby area dominated by bramble which produces some fruit in the autumn. There are several hundred different species of brambles, so it is hardly surprising that some bushes seem to produce better blackberries than others. Compare the leaves and you may find two or three different types in one small patch.

Continue downhill, cross a footbridge and turn left down the road and past Rakefoot Farm. About 100m past the farm entrance is a signpost to Spring Farm. Turn left down to a stile and go over this, then across the field and over a footbridge. Turn right and follow the beck downstream.

There is a bank of woodland still to the right, mostly of ash and beech. These two

trees rarely grow together except where they have been deliberately planted. Ash produces a light and dappled shade, beneath which plants like the celandine and anemone can flourish, whilst beech forms a dense dark canopy offering few opportunities for 'vernal' (spring) flowers.

Go over a stile and along the narrow path with the stream still to your right. After crossing a second stile turn left, waymarked 'Great Wood', and continue to another stile leading into the wood. Follow the path down between the trees, ignoring any right turns; continue to a junction with a vehicle track and follow this, still obliquely down-hill.

Mostly larch trees now, but there are mossy oak stumps here and there, for much of the year acting as headstones in a quiet wood-land graveyard. A few flowers have survived the transition, including the wood sorrel, its small shamrock-shaped leaves often carpeting the banks. Wood sorrel was once used as the basis for a sauce or as part of a salad; try a single leaf, sharp and refreshing, but not recommended in large doses.

Carry on south-west, bearing right when the car park comes into view.

The north-east shore of Derwent Water, Keswick to the top right

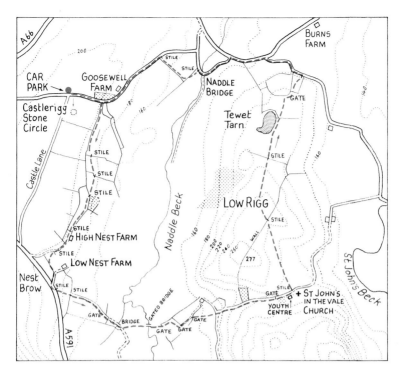

Walk Four
NADDLE VALLEY
& LOW RIGG

CASTLERIGG — ST JOHN'S IN THE VALE CHURCH — TEWET TARN; 6km

A walk of great charm rather than grandeur, a combination of low fell and green pasture in which pastoral elements are strong, though the 'Out with Romany' impression of pre-war simplicity is misleading.

Park at GR 292237, on the roadside opposite the entrance to Castlerigg stone circle.

Start with a detour; the route goes along the road and straight past the entrance to the stone circle, but it is impossible to pass by without walking up the field to stand among the stones. Father West, writing in the 18th century, described it as a 'wide circle of rude stones; the awful monument of the barbarous superstition which enslaved the minds of ancient times'. This assessment may have been far from objective, but in truth nobody really knows what stone circles were for.

The Castlerigg or Keswick Stones were put into place in the Bronze Age, probably about 3,000 years ago; there are 48 of them and they are not quite in a circle. Fact then gives way to fantasy, and a host of theories have been put forward to account for such megaliths, the most bizarre being that they were galactic computers, constructed of macro rather than micro chips. The area around the stone circle was once cultivated, a fact revealed by the surrounding ridge and furrow marks. This suggests that our

25

Castlerigg Stone Circle

more recent ancestors were less impressed by the monument than by the comparatively level ground which could be used for crops.

From the gate go east along the roadside, i.e. right when facing the road from the gate.

The hedgerow is remarkably rich in herbs. Some of these, such as woundwort and herb robert, are typical of uncut road verges everywhere, but there are others like wood sorrel and herb bennet which are woodland species and rarely colonise open ground. So this hedge may be the skeleton of an ancient coppice: the variety of trees and bushes (ash, hazel, wych elm etc.) would make it a likely explanation, and it is a pity it has been so badly neglected.

Continue along the roadside until a footpath marked 'The Nest' leads right. Go down the field and make for a stone stile in the wall.

The plantation to the left provides a shelterbelt, a narrow ribbon of trees just wide enough to offer protection to stock in severe weather and to accommodate pheasants for winter shooting. The upper part has been replanted and will be allowed

to mature before another section is cut down. This provides continuous cover whilst allowing a crop of trees to be harvested.

Go through the stile, bearing slightly left and to the left of a bend or kink in the wall ahead. Go through another stile into a third field, this time making for a ladder stile in the right-hand corner, alongside a small plantation.

The trees are mostly pine and larch, again maintained as shelter for stock.

Follow the path to the right of a hedge. This is replaced by a wall as you approach High Nest Farm.

To the right of the path are several sturdy hazel trees, though 'trees' is perhaps the wrong word; bushes might be more accurate. This is as big as they ever seem to get and their natural habitat is as a shrub growing beneath taller trees. Hazel gets its name from the Anglo-Saxon 'haesel', meaning 'command', and wands or sticks of hazel were used long before teachers discovered canes.

Go through the gate and onto a metalled track.

This is High Nest, full of fascinating details; past the byre try to find the unusual 'date mark', the vine, the toadflax on the wall. An engaging and apparently ageless world, yet vulnerable to every breath of change.

Continue down the tarmac drive to a stile on the left just before a cattle grid. Cross the stile and walk down the field. Bear a little to the right, to make for a cattle grid on another metalled track below. At the track bear right, with Low Nest Farm to the left, towards a main road.

The hedge to the right, bearing honeysuckle and wild raspberry, is yet another ancient one; the clue this time is wood horsetail, growing on both sides of the track and resembling a finely-structured garden horsetail.

Horsetails have come through the last few hundred million years with little change to their structure. They are closely related to ferns and bear 'cones' rather than flowers, and produce spores rather than seeds. Years ago, before brillo pads were invented, horsetails were used to clean pots and pans. Feel the stem and you can understand why, though the type sold for scouring pads was of a different species and much coarser than the wood horsetail.

The roughness of the stem is caused by tiny deposits of silica (as in sandpaper), a useful adaptation to put-off hungry insects and sheep.

At the main road (on Nest Brow) turn left, and, after 50m, go left at a stile. Cross the field to another stile through a tall drystone wall.

An excellent place to look over the Naddle valley towards High Rigg. The sides of the green and fertile valley end abruptly, meeting the bracken-covered lower fells at a stone wall without any intermediate enclosures or 'intake'. This gives the impression that the fell is neatly contained, like a film-set for the well-known fairy story about a magic cooking pot which buries a village in a great dome of lumpy porridge. Fossilised porridge is perhaps an apt description for the present appearance of the glaciated volcanic rock which forms the fell, but it hardly does justice to its scenic qualities. It is probably a gigantic 'roche

moutonnée', shaped by ice moving over its surface.

From the stile go left and then right around the field edge, following the boundary down to a gate. Go through this and along the farm track.

To the left is a marshy area, the ideal habitat for snipe. During the spring they can be heard 'drumming' overhead, a sound created by air vibrating through the outer tail feathers as the bird descends in a display flight. The sound carries a surprising distance and, like the song of the skylark, seems to fill the sky without any point of origin.

Reed grass

The small group of birch trees beyond the fence provides a feeding ground for that most beautiful of game birds, the woodcock. Both snipe and woodcock are shot at but they are extremely difficult to hit. A much more efficient method of catching woodcock for the pot was employed by local poachers; this was a trap known as a 'sprint', an ingenious device involving a line of stones with a gap in the middle across which was set a snare. Woodcock dislike stepping over stones and prefer to look for a convenient gap or gateway.

Walk along the track to a small footbridge over the drainage channel. Bear left just after the bridge, off the track and onto a grassy path. Head towards a white-gated footbridge over the Naddle Beck.

The water is fast and clear with submerged clumps of crowfoot (a sort of aquatic buttercup with white petals) and a border of reed grass.

There are few clues here to the schizophrenic nature of upland streams, usually friendly but capable of ferocious violence. Even the benign becks flanking High Rigg are capable of occasional outbursts. In 1749 there was a memorable storm when 'the inhabitants of the vale [of St John's] heard a strange buzzing noise . . . for two hours together, before the breaking of the clouds . . Catchety Gill swept away a mill and a kiln in five minutes, leaving the place where they stood covered by huge rocks and rubbish, three or four yards deep'. This must have been unusual even by Lake District standards because the inhabitants 'who were scarce less astonished . . than they would have been at the sound of the last trumpet . . climbed the neighbouring tree, and others got on top of hay stacks'. The fields on the valley floor are mostly down to hay or pasture, an indication that flooding still prevents arable crops from being grown with any confidence.

Continue across the bridge and along the path for about 50m to a wicket gate by the side of a five-bar gate. Go through this and across the next field by keeping close to the fence on your left. A wicket gate then leads to the left up a farm track.

The fields are rather more varied here,

perhaps kale or a root crop grown as fodder for Friesian cattle. The pasture is rich too, a mixture of grass and clover providing much better food value and ultimately a good milk yield.

After about 100m leave the track for a wicket gate on the right and continue straight on over rocky outcrops (cairned) to a metalled road.

Looking to the right it is now worth remembering the view across from Nest Brow; this is the meeting point between fell and pasture and it is marked by a very definite boundary wall. The terrain changes completely too, back onto familiar rocks and pebbles.

Follow the track as it climbs steeply, then levels out before approaching the grounds of Carlisle Diocesan Youth Centre and a small plantation of trees.

Before reaching the gates, look right to the open fells. Two small trees attract attention, apparently growing out of shallow rock faces on the exposed hillside. They are rowans, a species noted for its resilience and magical power. According to Icelandic legend, Thor was saved from the swollen waters of the River Vimur by catching hold of a rowan, and in Britain stories abound in the north and west about the protection afforded by a rowan branch. But not in the south of England, where it is a tree of suburban gardens and is known as the mountain ash. Presumably its lonely appearance on high hills in the uplands singled it out as a force against evil, protecting the byre and buttery from witchcraft.

The greatest threat to any vegetation on the fells is sheep, and the reason these rowans have escaped their attention is because sheep cannot climb cliffs. Heather and bilberry survive in much the same fugitive way.

Go through the gates and past the Youth Centre. Just beyond it, and almost completely hidden from view, is a church.

This is the church of St John's in the Vale; go through the gate for a walk around the churchyard, which has several interesting

A Friesian in search of better pasture; the Naddle Valley in June

features. The present building dates back only as far as 1845 but there has been a structure of some kind here for much longer.

There is a mysterious well towards the south-west corner, overshadowed by a canopy of yew, holly and rhododendron. Interesting to speculate on how many weary travellers drank from the cup and what unpleasant germs they picked up as a result.

The gravestones bear familiar local names, folk born and raised in the parish. The only wanderers commemorated are the Edmondsons who found their way to South Africa, America and Argentina, at a time when most of their neighbours probably thought Carlisle was a frontier post.

There is also a stone dedicated to John Richardson, a dialect poet of the 19th century who taught at the adjacent school, of which there is now no trace.

When you have finished looking at the fronts of the headstones try looking at the backs, where the clean air has enabled a riot of lichens to transform them into an abstract picture gallery.

From the church cross the road and go over a stile, onto the open fell. Bear slightly to the right, keeping the higher ground to the left and making for a distant wall. The path becomes more distinct as you continue north.

Skiddaw is ahead, with Blencathra much more obvious to the right. Quarries scar the lower slopes of Threlkeld Knotts to the east, culminating to the north-east in the famous Threlkeld Quarries which extract micro-granite from what is probably a laccolith — an intrusion pushed up into a dome beneath the older rock. Unlike good quality slate, granite is only worth quarrying if there is immediate access to a road system for cheap transport.

At the wall, go through the stile. Again the way is not clear on the ground; bear ahead and slightly right, through the shallow gap

29

with Low Rigg to your right. Bear right, making for the right of Tewet Tarn which should now be visible to the north. Cross a fence in the dip via a stile to the left, then continue over the ridge, still making for the right of the tarn.

Tewet Tarn, known locally as Tewfit Tarn, is very shallow and has a reputation for freezing early and providing skating practice. 'Tewet' is a colloquial name for lapwing and describes the call of the bird just as well as the more widespread 'peewit'. Try to think of other birds named after their call and you may find it surprisingly difficult. In fact there are four or five, including obscure ones like 'oriole' and obvious ones like 'cuckoo'.

A wall lies ahead. Go over the stile, about 80m up from the tarn, then continue straight ahead (north) for about 100m to a rocky knoll with a wooden signpost.

There are hawthorn bushes just before the knoll, nibbled by generations of sheep into some very strange shapes. The only reason the bushes survive is the protection afforded by their thorns, which deter sheep from trying to reach the new leaf growth.

Bear right alongside a wall; follow this as it turns left, then go through a gate and diagonally right, down a field to the road. Go through the gate and left along the road.

To the right is Blencathra, its elegant saddleback rising to 868m (2,848ft). The high plateau of Mungrisdale Common and Skiddaw Forest stretch beyond, hidden from view but the nearest thing to wilderness that the Lake District has to offer.

In the foreground is Burns Farm. Around the old core are several new buildings added over recent years to house machinery or stock. To the left is a silage clamp, a feature appearing more and more in upland farms. To winter stock requires a great deal of fodder: hay is too unreliable (requiring dry weather for successful harvesting), so silage-making was introduced. Instead of needing a dry haystack, grass for silage is chopped up and rolled in a great pit or clamp with black plastic draped over the top to keep air out. Old tyres are usually used to weight the plastic down; not

very attractive, but efficient. Apart from the obvious visual change, the disadvantage with silage in lowland England is that it is cut earlier than hay, so meadow flowers do not get a chance to produce seed and soon disappear; hence no cowslips. In the Lake District silage is often cut at about the same time as hay, and the chief conservation problem is not the loss of flowers but the increased pollution caused by the massive increase in the use of nitrogenous fertilisers for silage crops.

At the junction turn left onto the main road, then first left again.

The bank to the left is covered with bracken and male fern; bracken used to be called lady or female fern and it is interesting to compare them and see what 19th century naturalists considered feminine.

Freud would have an explanation of course, particularly for Victorian entomologists who discovered dowdy little moths and gave them names like true lovers knot and maiden's blush.

The road bears right, over a bridge.

This is Naddle Bridge; look to the right where there is an alder grove and a sloe thicket. The thorny cover attracts birds like buntings and warblers which are able to nest in comparative safety. Their chief predator here is the stoat which is a very efficient hunter and is capable of reaching any nest built close to the ground.

There is a gate and a stile on the left side of the road about 30m after the bridge. Go through the stile bearing right across the corner of the field, then through a gateway and across the corner of the next field to a gate. Turn right before the gate and follow the edge of the field uphill to a stile. Go over the stile and turn left along the road.

The road passes Goosewell Farm, another fascinating group of buildings with an old whitewashed byre set amid modern storage and stock sheds. Don't be too surprised to see a peacock around the place — farmers often keep unusual pets.

Continue along the road, up the hill and back to the car park.

Walk Five
CAT BELLS

GUTHERSCALE — CAT BELLS — MANESTY PARK — BRANDELHOW — HAWES END; 6.5km

Visitors to Keswick and Derwent Water are quickly seduced by the distinctive features of Cat Bells, and it is one of the most popular of all the minor fells. The route suggested here includes the ridge and peak of Cat Bells, involving two sharp gradients but sublime views, returning via beautiful parkland on the lake's shore.

Cat Bells with Derwent Water to the left

Start at GR 246212. Park at Gutherscale car park, reached by following the Grange road for 3km south of Portinscale. From the car park follow the side road back towards Keswick.

After a few metres the trees to the left give way to a surprisingly good view both north and west. Skiddaw dominates the skyline above Portinscale and Keswick. It is formed of soft grey shale and siltstone which weather easily in frost and rain, so that there is no craggy peak but many cascades of fine scree. Most of the final shaping of this landscape came not from glaciers during the Ice Age but from 'periglacial' activity, the period of freezing and thawing that followed in its wake.

Closer at hand is the dome of Swinside, clothed in a coniferous plantation of pine, larch and spruce and, across the Newlands Beck, the treeless whaleback of Barrow. Just left of the scree area beneath the flanks of Barrow is Farm Uzzicar, named after Husaker Tarn. The tarn was drained in the 13th century but the 'new lands' reclaimed in the process still provide a name for the whole valley.

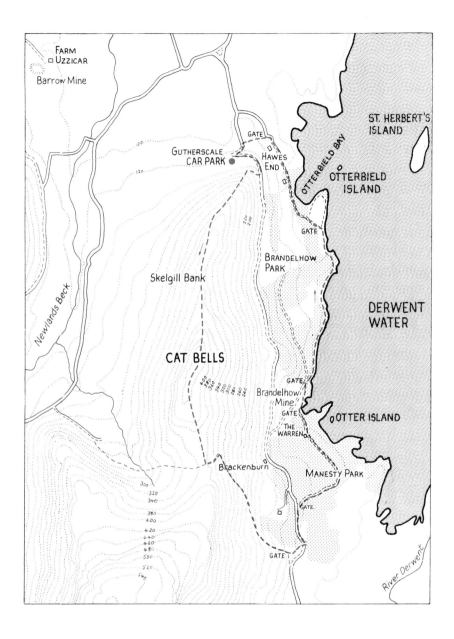

At the junction with the main road bear right, along the Grange road. After about 100m, opposite a sign marked 'Cat Bells ridge', bear right, up a trackway.

The wide track and erosion show how popular the route is. The most common plant here is bracken, but foxglove is also characteristic. Trampling prevents it from flowering, and the broad leaves are not so obvious as the tall flowering spikes. Foxglove, known by all sorts of nicknames such as 'thimbles' and 'deadmen's bellows', contains a toxin called digitalin. In very minute doses it is used medicinally to treat certain heart complaints, but like so many traditional cures it can be lethal in large doses.

32

After about 50m a smaller path turns sharp right, off the main track. Follow this as it zig-zags up onto the ridge.

It is tempting to stop on one of the 'false peaks' along Skelgill Bank. Take the opportunity to look out over Derwent Water. The islands in particular demand attention; the nearest is Otterbield. 'Bield' means 'place of shelter', but otters are uncommon in Cumbria now and are unlikely to return to such an exposed retreat. Behind Otterbield is St Herbert's Island. Herbert was a 7th century hermit who believed in the contemplative life. He was a close friend of St Cuthbert, the popular Bishop of Lindisfarne who also spent a remarkable amount of his time on small islands, such as Hobthrush (off Holy Island) and Farne. The saints met once a year, presumably to exchange prayers rather than gossip, and died on the same day in 678. Beyond St Herbert's is Rampsholme Island, and further left towards the far shore are Lord's Island and Derwent Isle — of which more on walk 2.

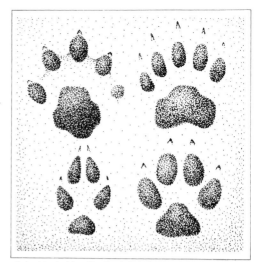

Animal footprints; otter (top left) badger (top right) fox (bottom left) and dog (bottom right)

Continue along the crest of the ridge, keeping to the worn path and avoiding the slippery grassed slopes.

Barrow will still be an obvious feature to the north-west. Find Farm Uzzicar again and you will see, a little to its left, the spoil heaps of Barrow Mine. Its most prosperous period was in the 1880s when there was a 60-foot wheel and a 20 horse-power steam engine. Prior to that in the middle of the 19th century it had been worked by a community of self-employed miners each paying a small tribute to the Keswick company. Many of these singular characters hoarded the ore (mostly galena, cerrusite and blende) and stored it in underground chambers, presumably so that they could retire early and live off the spoils. A miner's life was hard and dangerous however, and over the years secret hoards have occasionally been discovered, suggesting that the rightful owners died before they could cash-in their savings.

Follow the path up to the top of Cat Bells (past the grass-covered remains of some very old mine workings on the ridge crest).

From Cat Bells the head of the Newlands valley looks incredibly verdant, hayfields and pasture sheltered in a lattice of tree-lined walls and hedges, the improved 'in-bye' land contrasting sharply with the bracken-covered fells. Most of the fields are the result of the great enclosure awards of the 18th and 19th centuries: before then there would have been a more open system of pasture and woodland, less obviously contained in the basin of the valley.

From the summit the path descends, still on the ridge, to a wide flat area before ascending again. Do not follow the path uphill again, but from the lowest point of the flat area turn left towards Derwent Water, downhill on the path guarded by rails. The path zig-zags steeply at first and then slants south-east until level with a wood on the left.

Badgers inhabit the nearby woods, and their tracks can sometimes be seen in muddy places on the fells where they have been out at night foraging for food. The footprint (emblem of the Cumbria Naturalists' Trust) is distinctive, broad and with five toes rather than the four associated with dog or fox prints. Badgers, known locally as 'pates' or 'grays', were virtually extinct in the Lake District by the end of the 18th century following a couple of centuries of persecution. A bounty of a shilling a head (literally) nearly finished them off but they have increased considerably this century, especially in the southern fells.

33

Continue alongside the wood (ignore paths joining from the left) to a gate, at which turn left onto a road. Walk left along the roadside for about 300m, then turn right along a metalled track which leads through a gate into Manesty Park.

Manesty, bought by the National Trust in 1905, is very Victorian. Their idea was that woodland should contain a variety of form, shape and colour, and since British trees often weren't up to the required standard, foreign ones brought back by adventurers were introduced. Fortunately, Borrowdale still has many pieces of unspoiled native woodland so it is possible to forgive former excesses and enjoy what is, in fact, a very attractive combination of oak and larch. Wordsworth hated larch trees, but they have the advantage of being deciduous (losing their needles in autumn), allowing some shrubs and flowers to grow in the dappled shade.

In theory most woods should have a shrub zone beneath the canopy, but often this is restricted by grazing animals like deer or sheep which eat anything within reach. The old holly bushes in Manesty Park have a browse line about a metre from the ground, suggesting there are plenty of sheep about with a taste for holly-prickles.

The metalled track leads through the wood to a slate-built house ('The Warren') on the left.

Otter Island — minus any otters — is just offshore in Abbot's Bay, screened by the trees to the right, and is well worth a detour

View from Cat Bells summit — south clockwise to north

for a better view. Back on the main route the track goes through an interesting marshy area with birch and willow trees (native and natural) and rhododendron (Himalayan and introduced).

Continue for about 200m, go through a five-bar gate and along the path between a house and garages, with old boathouses to the right.

There is an extensive area of mine waste just after the house; this is what remains of the Brandley or Brandelhow Mine, dating back many hundreds of years and one of the oldest in the Lake District. It was a lead mine, yielding galena and cerussite, but also some blende (zinc sulphide) and even a little silver and gold. The problem was water, which eventually defeated every effort to keep the shafts open, including the introduction of a steam engine in the middle of the 19th century.

After crossing the mine waste bear left and follow the fence for a few metres before going through the gate to the right and into Brandelhow Park.

This was the first property bought by the National Trust in the Lake District. The Trust was founded in 1895 and its first secretary, Canon Rawnsley, was vicar of Crosthwaite, just west of Keswick. He knew Brandelhow very well and its acquisition for the nation in 1900 must have given him a great deal of satisfaction.

This path must also have been walked regularly by Hugh Walpole, who lived at

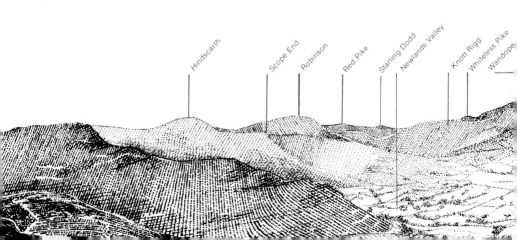

Brackenburn a little way to the south-west, for it is the most direct route from there to the shore of Derwent Water. Walpole was a prolific novelist and wrote several long stories *(The Herries Chronicle)* set in Borrowdale and Keswick, but most literary critics are now dismissive about his work. His name, nearly household in the 1920s and 30s, is now virtually forgotten.

Brandelhow is rather different to Manesty; there are some majestic Douglas firs and these seem particularly attractive to squirrels; not grey squirrels but the native and much more endearing red. They are noisy animals, chasing each other from tree to tree or dropping cones from overhead branches and chattering with agitation. They are not always easy to see however, and patience is not always rewarded. During the autumn and winter red squirrels have a blackish or dark brown tail, but by the following summer this has been bleached almost white. The coat is moulted twice a year but the ear tufts and the tail once only — hence a sudden change from white to black.

Follow the well-worn track and, when a smaller path bears right, go down to the waterside; a path leads parallel with the shore.

Derwent Water is very shallow compared with most other Cumbrian lakes. When the great ice sheets melted at the end of the Ice Age (the 'retreat' of the Ice Age) they dumped an equally great amount of silt and debris, which filled up the wide valley of the Derwent. Bassenthwaite Lake and Derwent Water were joined for a long time, and the land separating them is still very low and marshy. Because it is so shallow (about 22m maximum) Derwent Water does not have any char, a fish characteristic of the deeper lakes. On the other hand both Derwent Water and Bassenthwaite have the vendace, an obscure little whitefish found nowhere else in England. After severe weather vendace are sometimes washed up on the shore, but that is about the only time that they are seen, for unlike the trout they do not rise to any bait.

The curious plant growing in the shallows is quillwort, a primitive non-flowering species most closely related to horsetail.

After several hundred metres of lakeside the path leads through a gate and into a field. The direct path goes left here, following the line of the wall, but a detour along the shore and around the small raised headland offers splendid views and adds little in distance.

Otterbield Bay lies just to the north of the headland, its indented shore collecting silt which in turn has allowed *Phragmites* reed to colonise the shallows. Reed beds are uncommon on most of the larger lakes, the main exception being Esthwaite (to the west of Windermere) which is much richer in nutrients.

Otterbield Island is again visible from the headland, with St Herbert's Island beyond. Beatrix Potter used St Herbert's Island as the setting for her story about Squirrel Nutkin, in which the squirrels boated out to Owl Island to collect hazel nuts.

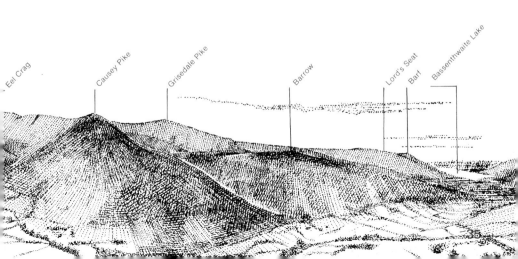

Eel Crag Causey Pike Grisedale Pike Barrow Lord's Seat Barf Bassenthwaite Lake

Leave the field via a track and raised walkway which bears right into another field. Continue along this path, bearing left when this divides and taking the higher level to pass close beneath a house and up to a metalled track. Turn right down the track, which passes to the right of Hawes End Centre. Continue for about 50m to a wicket gate on the wooded bank to the left.

The commonest bird along the civilised borders of Derwent Water is the chaffinch, which has become accustomed to the easy living provided by tourists. Chaffinches sit in the trees overhead waiting for people to drop crumbs or uncover seeds on the ground, and in many respects they behave like diminutive vultures. They can be recognised by the white bars on their wings and shoulders, and by their call which has earned them their local name 'spink'.

Go through the gate and bear right, around a grassy knoll to meet a drystone wall. Turn left to meet the road, at which turn left again and walk over a cattle grid to a road junction, then along the road and back to the car park.

The south-west shore of Derwent Water, Otter Island in the foreground

Walk Six
NEWLANDS VALLEY

CHAPEL BRIDGE — LOW SNAB — SKELGILL — LITTLE TOWN; 6.5km

It is possible to split this walk into two halves and take these independently (see map, page 38). The upper section of Newlands Valley is very beautiful but difficult of access, and the route suggested is one of the few that keeps to the level valley without suddenly launching itself onto a ridge or steep stream-side. Instead, it concentrates on hay meadows and pasture below the mine-scarred hills of Scope End, Maiden Moor and Cat Bells.

Park on the road verge on the east side of Chapel Bridge, GR 233194, just south of Little Town. Walk over the bridge and go through the gate to the left after about 50m.

There are drystone walls on either side, covered with the coloured spots and dabs of lichens, especially *Lecanora* (white), *Candelariella* and *Xanthoria* (yellow). Lichens are very singular plants; they live for a very long time, can withstand considerable periods of drought, are very sensitive to pollution, and are used in the preparation of dyes and antibiotics. The most curious thing about them, however, is that they function by a form of symbiosis (team work) in which fungi create the outer shell and framework and algae make the food. This complicated arrangement was discovered in the last century by Beatrix Potter.

Walk along the track towards a small church.

Just before the church on the right is a gateway with a 'slope stone', a slate slab with holes in it to take the wooden rails or beams that preceded gates.

Newlands Church is very pretty, mid-European in appearance, painted white and surrounded by sycamore trees enclosed by a neat stone wall. The tiny schoolroom to the left was added just over a century ago but was closed (as a school) in 1967.

Take the left turn, opposite the church, marked as a private road to Low Snab.

The view to the right includes Causey Pike, its unusual cone-tipped summit rising to 617m (2,035ft). To its left are Scar Crags, weathered dramatically into a series of acute ridges and grooves like the heading of a curtain.

Ahead, the valley of the Newlands Beck forks, Scope Beck going off to the right and the main beck continuing due south. Between them lies Scope End, leading upwards to the considerable summit of Hindscarth.

The road goes over a small bridge; go straight on, through the gate, alongside a field and through another gate towards Low Snab Farm.

This is one of the most attractive views of a Lakeland farm in its timeless setting. The slopes of Scope End are grazed by Herdwick sheep from the farm; the nearest neighbour to the south-west is Gatesgarth (by Buttermere), and the distance between the two farms is about 6km.

Apart from the sheep the farm also has a small herd of Ayrshire cattle, kept for their milk. They are preferred to the more usual Friesians because they are less bulky and easier to manage in the small byre.

Go through the gate (close it carefully) and through the farm, taking care not to disturb any work in progress.

Most old farms in the area date back to the period between 1650 and 1750 and have been shaped by function and climate since then. The farmhouse is to the right, the byre and hay barn to the left. High up in

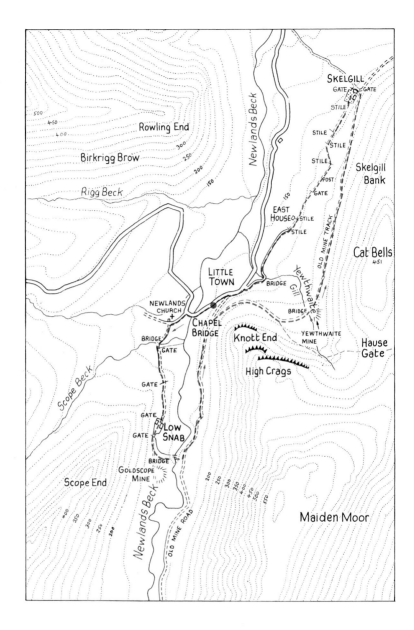

the wall above the byre door is an old pigeon loft, a rare feature in Lakeland and a legacy from the days when there was little fresh meat in the winter and a pigeon pie or two came in handy. This was in the 17th and 18th centuries when farmers could not provide enough hay for their sheep and some of the flock had to be slaughtered in the autumn. The carcasses were cut into 'collops' and hung in open chimneys to smoke dry, a process commemorated in 'Collop Monday' when children were allowed a special feast on the Monday preceding Lent.

Go through the gate at the far end of the farm and continue with the wall to your left.

The great mound of spoil to the right is from the Goldscope Mine, first mentioned in the 13th century and subsequently one of the most productive of all the Lakeland mines. Two parallel veins of lead were worked, running north-east to south-west, of which the east lode was up to 4.2m thick. Diagonal to this was a rich 2.7m vein of copper, and there was some silver and some gold also. Little wonder that the Germans who developed the mine called it 'Gottes Gaab' (i.e. God's gift), a name the locals soon corrupted to Goldscope.

The mine finally closed operations in the middle of the 19th century. Apart from the huge heaps of spoil the only visible features remaining are the adits or entrances, called the Pan Holes, on the slope of Scope End.

The wall bears left; follow the path which leads parallel with the wall and down to a bridge over the beck.

There is still quite a lot of surface debris to the right, but it is sobering to see that the only monument to hundreds of years of human endeavour is an unsightly scatter of rubble. Some information about the mine can be deduced from old records, but the story of the social and working conditions has probably been lost for ever.

Ahead are the steep slopes of Maiden Moor, whilst to the right the beck leads south to the 749m (2,473ft) peak of Dale Head, flanked by High Spy to the east and Hindscarth to the west. The rocky buttress jutting out on the left side of the valley is called Castle Nook.

Continue over the bridge to join a main track after about 100m.

This is the old mine road leading to Castle - nook Mine and Dale Head; the copper mine at Dale Head was opened at the turn of the 17th century by Daniel Hechstetter, a name that crops up time and time again in the Elizabethan exploitation of the Lake District mines. Most were subsequently closed either by force or by indirect pressure in the English Civil War, but many had a second lease of life during the Industrial Revolution.

Turn left and walk along the track.

Drystone walls like the one on the left are used as shelter by many small mammals

such as voles and weasels. These rarely show themselves, however, and the only creature likely to be seen coming out of a wall crevice is a wren. This tiny bird not only nests among the stones but also finds enough insect food there to keep it alive throughout the winter. Most insectivorous birds migrate, but the wren always stays in its own territory and risks starvation if weather is severe. After two or three mild winters the wren becomes the commonest bird in Britain with up to ten million breeding pairs, but numbers can crash dramatically, especially in high fell country where alternative habitats are limited.

Wren

The view to the left is of the beautiful upper section of the Newlands valley: hay meadows, farms, and tree-lined hedges. On the steep south-facing slopes of the adjacent fells can be seen two carpets of trees, the famous Keskadale and Birkrigg oaks. These small woods climb to an altitude of about 500m and are thought to be at the limit of the tree's climatic range in this country. They have much in common with Wistman's Wood on Dartmoor but are composed of sessile rather than pedunculate oak. Whilst many of the Bor-rowdale woods were planted, there is little doubt that these curious stunted and deformed trees are the descendants of the original canopy that existed more than 7,000 years ago.

Just before the track bears right, and with Chapel Bridge across the field to the left, there is a green path which angles up through bracken to the right, below a small crag. If you wish to complete the whole walk (a distance of another 4km) take this path.

If, however, you wish to finish the walk at this point keep to the main track for a few more metres, then turn left down the bank and to the wall end, over a stile at the fence, and left to the car park.

Assuming that you have decided to continue . . . . follow the green path which angles right to join another old mine track, at which continue right.

Ahead on the east side of the Newlands valley is Cat Bells (see walk 5) with the wooded dome of Swinside to the north: to the immediate right is Knott End, the lowest of a triple tier of crags rising via High Crags to Maiden Moor. The west side of Newlands has not yet resolved itself and is dominated by Birkrigg Brow and Rowling End, on the shoulder of Causey Pike.

Continue along the track, bearing right, with the settlement of Little Town to the left. There is now a wall to the left and the track straightens.

The coll or cleft in the ridge between Cat Bells and Maiden Moor is called Hause Gate, 'Hause' meaning a pass.

The untidy mounds on the left bank of Yewthwaite Gill are what remains of Yewthwaite Mine, worked first in the mid-18th century. It was very profitable compared with most other local mines, partly because the shafts were shallow and the ore was easy to extract, requiring a minimum of equipment. Like many mines it suffered closure, only to be reopened and reworked in the mid-19th century. At its peak it was producing 426 tonnes per year: cerrusite, galena and pyrites, worth nearly £6,000 — a fortune for the owner considering the small overheads.

The track follows the wall to the left, then leads over a bridge.

This is Yewthwaite Gill, though at this point the stream itself is usually subterranean. There is spoil above and below the track; a little way beyond the bridge (turning left then bearing right) is an interesting cobbled yard, the most visual evidence of what must once have been a bustling, noisy place.

From the deserted working continue north-north-east for several hundred metres along the track, with the steep slope of Cat Bells to the right.

Beatrix Potter knew this area very well in the late 19th and early 20th centuries; she visited Little Town several times on holiday and staged the story of Mrs Tiggywinkle on the meadows and the lower slopes of Cat Bells. The door of Mrs Tiggywinkle's house is somewhere amongst the bracken to the right of the path, a magical spot the exact location of which was known only to Beatrix Potter, and perhaps to Lucy of Little Town who followed the hedgehog looking for her 'pocket-hankins and her pinny'. Beatrix Potter did much more for the Lake District than write children's stories however; she was a well-respected naturalist who did a great deal of work on fungi (she illustrated a definitive book about toadstools), and with the royalties from her books she bought hundreds of acres of land which she donated to the National Trust.

Eventually the track descends, with the buildings of Skelgill to the left. Turn left onto the road and go through the gate, then bear right in front of the white house. Turn left off the road, along a path and through the gate to the right of this house. This leads through a small plantation of trees to a gate; go over the stile next to this gate and along the green path heading south-west.

Down the hill to the right is an old farm, probably dating back to the late 17th century when the 'long-house' was popular. This allowed the farmer to be under the same roof as his cattle, though why he found this so desirable is a mystery. The smell of cattle was once thought to ward off disease, so perhaps the legendary longevity of farmers was due to ammonia rather than to regular exercise.

Follow the grassy path across the rough pasture and meadowland, crossing two stiles over fences and a ladder stile over a wall. The path then bears slightly right, away from the hedge, making for a post marking the gap through an old field boundary. From here the path continues to the left of a derelict hedge, goes through a wicket gate and follows a ridge (another old field boundary), still heading south-west.

The traditional field system has long fallen into disuse and the hawthorn hedges are almost moribund, though the old banks harbour many wild flowers.

Newlands Church, with Little Town and Cat Bells in the distance

The grassland is predominantly of the 'bent/fescue' type, i.e. *Agrostis* and *Festuca* grasses with occasional crested dogstail, cocksfoot etc. On good ground most fields are planted with better quality grasses like timothy, but gradually even these give way to 'weed' species offering a poorer yield.

Ahead is Little Town at the foot of Maiden Moor, with Scope End in the distance, backed by Dale Head to the left and Robinson to the right. The latter, a peak of 732m (2,417ft) commemorates Richard Robinson who once owned it; immortality in place-names is fickle and one would have expected someone to come up with a more descriptive name in subsequent centuries.

Continue for several hundred metres, crossing old hedge-lines and small streams, **and passing a cottage ('East House') to the right. Go over the stile to the right of a gate, then cross the corner of the field to another stile, leading to a trackway. Walk along the trackway which bears left, over a bridge.**

This is Yewthwaite Gill again, which meets Newlands Beck a little way to the north-west. Newlands Beck eventually feeds into Bassenthwaite Lake. The fields in this area are more functional: for much of the year they hold Swaledale ('Swaddle') sheep or store cattle. The latter are very demanding on winter feed but they are not selective grazers and improve the quality of the pastures by eating-off the less palatable rushes and coarse grasses.

The track bears right to meet the road, at which turn left, through Little Town, and down to the car park.

41

Walk Seven
CASTLE CRAG

ROSTHWAITE — LOW HOWS WOOD — CASTLE CRAG; 5km

The superb view from Castle Crag is the main object of the exercise, but there is a lot to be seen on the way, especially on the attractive river Derwent and its associated woods and pastures. Much of the route is over gentle terrain, but the final approach is steep and stony and requires some care.

Park at Rosthwaite, either on the roadside on the Keswick (north) side of the village GR 258149, or at a walled car park up the metalled track opposite the Post Office (the end house). The walk begins on this track, heading west away from the road. The track leads to Yew Tree Farm then bears slightly right.

The walls of the farm buildings are of grey slate interwoven with rounded boulders picked from the riverside. Look at the corner of the hay barn on the right; the slates are 'watershot', meaning they are angled downwards so that any rain blown into the gaps runs out again. Minor features like this have been evolved over centuries of hard-earned experience. Hay needs to be kept well ventilated but dry, so a constant through-flow of air is provided by a slatted 'window' on the western face of the building. The roof is of local slate, hard-wearing but difficult to cleave, large heavy pieces at the base decreasing in size to the apex, totally unlike the uniform materials encouraged by modern builders.

Carry on down the gravel track, with stone walls on either side.

Just over the wall on the right is a curious low wooden roof hiding an equally curious concrete structure, a sheep dip, though the dip itself is lost among the various accessories such as the forcing pen, designed to sort out the sheep and to regulate proceedings.

At one time sheep were 'salved' with a mixture of tar and butter, believed to 'promote the growth of wool, and enable the fleece to better resist the wet'. These days a dip suffices; there are many unpleasant parasites on the fells trying to get under the fleece of sheep, so dipping is an essential seasonal exercise involving the use of a strong organophosphorus pesticide. Dieldrin used to be used, but it was banned in 1965 because it was having a drastic effect on wildlife. Predators like the peregrine falcon fed on other birds that had picked up the poison, and the cumulative concentration resulted either in death or sterility. Following the ban imposed on the really nasty pesticides (called organo-chlorides), the peregrine population has undergone a spectacular recovery and there are now pairs on most suitable Lakeland crags.

At the river bear right, keeping to the riverside track towards a bridge.

A straight, swift-running reach of the Derwent with a deep central channel, its volume of water depending on rainfall over Seathwaite Fell to the south-west.

A pair of dippers usually holds a territory here and can often be seen flying to and fro, low over the water. Dippers look like giant wrens but their characteristic white 'bib' is only visible when viewed head-on, and the chestnut-brown back and short whirring wings are often the best clues. Dippers are noisy birds; they have a loud call ('clink') and a curious song. This is best heard during the winter, because the dipper is one of the earliest nesting birds and is feeding young when most other species are just getting down to selecting sites.

Cross the packhorse bridge and bear right, following the river north on its west side.

Just after the bridge on the right is a small enclosure of oak, ash and rowan, planted with an eye to the future. No naturally-set seedlings can survive the constant grazing, so the 'generation gap' of trees has to be bridged by artificial means.

Go through the gate and bear right; continue parallel to the river. The track makes for the left of a tree-covered knoll before heading north-east to High Hows Wood.

The river is still close by. High Hows Wood is of very varied structure: oak, birch and hazel, ash, rowan and holly. Close to the river there

The river is to the right, screened by a small knoll and a healthy covering of shrubs and small trees. This type of vegetation is ideal for birds like the willow warbler which are hidden from view amongst the foliage, but can find an ample supply of insect food. Bird-watchers find these conditions particularly frustrating because the birds fly about continually and rarely offer a good view for identification; Wordsworth must have had this in mind when he wrote

'Alas! the fowls of heaven have wings.'

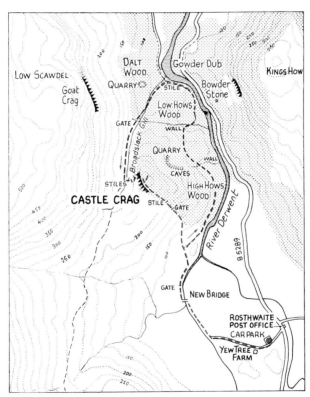

are also alders, not easy to describe except that the leaves are dark green with a blunt or indented end rather than a point. Alders are always associated with water and their orange seeds, dispersed from small round cones, are often carried downstream to be eaten by ducks, finches, mice or, a chance in a million, to grow into another tree.

A well-defined path leads through the wood, with an attractive rocky bank of oaks to the left, before descending to a flat area of marshland and scrub.

Most insectivorous birds arrive from Africa in April however, so there are a few weeks at the start of each breeding season when oakwoods have not grown sufficient leaf cover to obscure everything and birdwatchers have an opportunity to tick-off specialities like the wood warbler and the pied flycatcher.

Continue along the path, past a wooden sign to Grange, then up to the left, through a tumbled-down wall to an old quarry.

There is a cave to the left, damp but shallow, and some old quarry spoil colonised by larch trees.

The path makes its way to the right past the heaps of slate debris and leads uphill back into the wood.

The high wooded crags and quarries often ring with the sound of jackdaws. In the late summer and autumn the birch a little further along the path on the left is colonised by fly agaric toadstools, bright red with white spots and the kind that appear in many fairy stories. Fly agaric belongs to the *Amanitas,* a group that includes death cap and destroying angel, our most deadly fungi. Most people in this country have a policy of not eating toadstools unless they are proved to be harmless, but in France this idea is reversed and everything is eaten unless it is known to be poisonous. Because the death cap looks so unremarkable it has been the cause of many fatalities, whilst fly agaric is distinctive and easy to avoid. In some European countries fly agaric is sprinkled with sugar and placed on windowsills to attract and poison flies, but it has also been used down the centuries as an hallucinating drug or stimulant, often with unfortunate consequences.

At a path junction turn right, descending to a gap in a drystone wall. Go through this and over a flat grassy clearing towards the river, then bear left to keep by the riverside.

In heavy rain this flat area on the river bend is turned into an island, a shallow ox-bow to the left linking with the main river and sending a stream of water over the raised pathway. The river is lined with alders, their seeds attracting redpolls and siskins.

The path gains height to a gap through the rocks, then leads to a stile and descends again towards a small footbridge.

A good place to stop for a few minutes, though the river bend is too accessible from Grange to make it secluded, and there is a by-road just across the river. This beautiful reach of the river Derwent is called Gowder Dub, 'dub' being a deep pool.

The neck of Borrowdale, opening out to north and south, is where local people are supposed by tradition to have built a great wall to try to stop the last cuckoo from leaving, taking with it the last of the summer. The cuckoo (or 'gowk') sailed just clear of the cam stones, and one of the Borrowdale farmers is supposed to have exclaimed that had they built the wall a little higher they would have caught it. Like so many good folk-tales this one is linked with several other places around Britain, but it has special relevance to this area where the inhabitants of the dale were once innocent victims of the sort of joke now associated with the Irish.

Turn left before the footbridge, going up a track signposted as a bridleway to Seatoller.

Low Hows Wood is to the left, Dalt Wood to the right across Broadslack Gill.

The track crosses by a footbridge to the other side of the gill, then heads to a gate and out of the wood.

View from Castle Crag summit — east clockwise to west

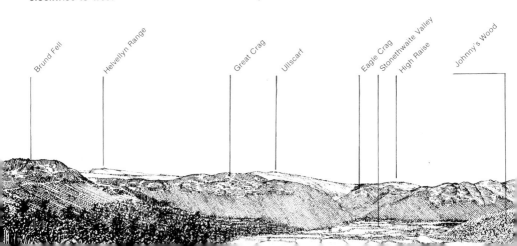

Brund Fell   Helvellyn Range   Great Crag   Ullscarf   Eagle Crag   Stonethwaite Valley   High Raise   Johnny's Wood

Derwent Water and Skiddaw, from Castle Crag. In the foreground are the densely wooded slopes of Borrowdale, obscuring the River Derwent

The old track was obviously well used by pack-ponies and was the main route to Rigghead Quarry, but has long been neglected. According to P.B.M. Allen such ancient by-ways have reverted 'to the use of the ghosts of those who made and used them'. Once out of the shadows and through the gate any unpleasant sensation should be dispelled by the view to the right, the rugged slope of Low Scawdel sprinkled with bonsai trees and bushes trying to make the most of thin pockets of soil.

Continue up the track, which is crossed by several small runners or streams, often culverted.

There is a sheep fold to the left, an essential enclosure used for centuries to assemble stock or provide shelter for ewes. The shape of the pen varies according to function, topography or tradition.

Glaramara   Great End   Seathwaite Valley   Scafell   Great Gable   High Scawdell   Goat Crag

Carry on to a flat grassy area with a large cairn, to the left of a stream crossing. Leave the track here and bear left, steeply uphill for about 50m to a wall stile, then to a ladder stile. Go over these and the fence immediately beyond, and take the zig-zagging path uphill.

A tiring last section towards the summit, and because of the slate (quarry waste again) the ascent should be taken carefully. Pine trees have managed to colonise the steep slope, showing that there is not a great deal of rock-slippage away from the path. Pine survives quite happily on thin dry soils, and it is possible that some of these trees are the descendants of post Ice-Age arrivals dating back more than 9,000 years, long before the oak trees took up residence.

The path leads to a flat grassy shelf with a cairn.

Alder leaves and Catkins

It is tempting to continue straight to the top, but stop awhile for the view south, unbeatable on a clear day when the river, green flat fields, walls and hedges, and the buildings of Rosthwaite crowd the foreground in fussy detail compared with the uncompromising peaks all around.

Take the path north, to the top of Castle Crag, just past the trees.

The summit cairn bears a dedication to the memory of John Harmer and ten other soldiers from Borrowdale, mostly of the Border Regiment, who fell in the Great War.

Derwent Water, with the iron-grey bulk of Skiddaw behind, is the focal point of the view north. Much closer is the village of Grange, which has an honourable history dating back at least to the monks of Furness who developed it as their abbey farm. Borrowdale was purchased by Furness from Alice de Rumelli in 1209, a holding extending from Sty Head and Great Gable to the south-west to Ashness and Dock Tarn to the north-east.

Just across the river Derwent to the right (east) is the Bowder Stone, a giant rock mostly obscured by trees but a favourite tourist attraction. Wordsworth, and Hutchinson before him, described it as resembling a stranded ship; their imagination was obviously keen and more ethereal than our own.

From the summit there is only one way down — the way that you came up. Cairns help to locate the top of the slate zig-zags. At the bottom cairn walk forward about 50m to a ladder stile over a wall close to some trees.

Obviously, ladder stiles have the advantage of not necessitating a gap in the wall, but they also avoid any contact with the stones and this means that the vital cap or camstones are not dislodged — the prelude by which walls begin to disintegrate. The making of drystone walls was a valued skill, now largely irrelevant in an age of barbed wire but still practised because landowners receive financial support to keep the characteristic landscape intact.

A proper drystone wall is broad at its base, has several 'through stones' (often slate) for support, and has its two faces infilled with rubble or 'hearting'. If it is not damaged by careless walkers a wall will last for at least a century, virtually free of maintenance.

Descend steeply left, parallel with the wall, to a wicket gate. The path then skirts left to begin a sinuous descent through open woodland to emerge by a fence gate to join the approach route. Retrace your steps alongside the Derwent to Rosthwaite.

Slate on Castle Crag ▷

Walk Eight
JOHNNY'S WOOD

SEATOLLER — JOHNNY'S WOOD — SCALECLOSE; 3.5km

A walk of two contrasting parts. The first is dominated by a marvellous Borrowdale oakwood flanked by the upper reaches of the river Derwent, the second by Scaleclose and Little Gatesgarthdale beneath High Scawdel and the shoulders of Dale Head and High Spy.

Start at Seatoller car park, GR 245138. Take the path to the left of the toilet block, between the farm buildings and, after 20m, bear right to a five-bar gate. Go through this into an open field.

To the right, beyond the stone wall and across the narrow valley are the Borrowdale Fells, a craggy and inhospitable block rising to Glaramara a little way to the south. The drystone walls in this district are all made from boulders collected from the riverside. Why bring slate from local quarries when an unending supply of ready-graded stone was available close at hand? Borrowdale folk were regarded as slow and backward by the sophisticated inhabitants of Keswick, but they were not stupid.

After about 50m a narrow path bears right, away from the main track. Take the smaller path with a drystone wall to the right. Continue to a wicket gate, through a wall on the right, and along the edge of the wood.

A group of holly trees lies just to the right of the path. Holly is dioecious, a term apparently invented by sadistic biology teachers who would have it pronounced dy-ee-shus, meaning that the male and female flowers are carried on different trees. In this group there is one male tree, producing enough pollen to ensure a fine show of winter berries on the neighbouring female trees.

Look closely at the holly leaves and you will notice that they are more prickly at the base than at the top, a defence against browsing animals. Also, many of the leaves have pale brown blotches on them, caused by the tiny grubs of leaf-mining flies called *Agromyzids* which tunnel into the leaves and feed on the soft inner tissue.

At the gap in the old wall bear left, to keep parallel with the river rather than going down to Folly Bridge. Continue alongside the wall to a five-bar gate leading back into Johnny's Wood. Go through the gate and down the track as it descends to the river, with a stone wall on the right and woodland to the left.

This is a hanging sessile oakwood, and a real charmer. Between great moss-strewn boulders and deep clefts the oaks usually manage to push up straight solid trunks, but their growth is clearly affected by the awkward conditions. There are two species of oak in Britain, and there is a general misconception that the sessile is suited to the rough slopes in the north and west whilst the pedunculate is the tree of the flat lowland plains. In fact although the sessile does show some preference for well-drained acid soils it would grow very well over most of England given the opportunity. Unfortunately it has suffered from a very bad reputation among nurserymen, and although sessile oak is a slower grower in its early years its mature timber is at least as good as that of the pedunculate. The lovely Borrowdale woods may not provide ideal conditions for timber but they are an ideal habitat for rare plants and animals, so much so that they are classified by the Nature Conservancy Council as 'clearly in the first echelon of Grade I sites'.

The track leads to a wicket gate. Go through this and bear left, over a rocky promontory by the river. The path levels out again once it is past the river bend.

Impressive, certainly, but sometimes the Derwent can be downright violent. Look at the far bank, in the process of being sliced away bit by bit to reveal great boulders amongst the glacial drift. The water has also sculpted hollows in the river bed and rarely allows rolling stones to stay around long enough to gather any aquatic moss.

wall corner. Continue to the left of the farm building and along another wooded section of the route.

This spot is particularly good for ferns, presumably because it is damp and heavily shaded. If you spend five minutes here you are bound to notice that there are many

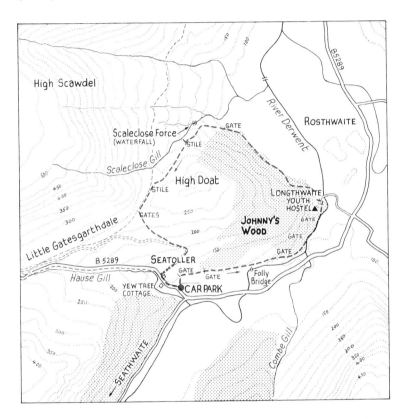

Upland reaches of rivers are uncomfortable places for plants and animals, but look for grey wagtails hawking for flies on the water's edge; they are finely-featured birds coloured grey, yellow, black and white, and are sufficiently common to be anticipated on most riverside walks.

Continue as the path heads north-east through another gate and into the grounds of Longthwaite Youth Hostel. Walk in front of the building and along the metalled track for a few metres. Where the track bears to the right however, you bear left, over the grass to make for a path to the left of the

different kinds. They include great filigree bunches of lady fern and, growing on tree stumps and in damp clefts, polypod and the exquisite beech fern, considered by many to be the most beautiful of them all. None transfer well to gardens, but the Victorians (who else?) went through a craze which saw several of the rarer species all but obliterated.

Continue along the stony track, with the wood to your left.

The fence is there to keep out sheep rather than humans. Grazing animals have prevented any regeneration of oak trees for

49

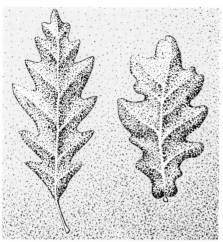
Leaves of sessile (left) and pedunculate oak

many years, but steps have been taken by the National Trust to plant young trees and protect them until they are past the palatable stage.

Until this century the Borrowdale woods, like those of Furness to the south, were worked as an economic concern and their coppices were managed with great care. When woodland products were no longer needed the coppices fell derelict and have been in a geriatric state ever since. Apart from the oak, hazel is the dominant tree. It rarely grows more than five or six metres tall and often goes unnoticed, but during the early spring, when the oak is still in tight bud, it opens out a flurry of catkins or 'lambs' tails' which respond to every breath of wind by delivering clouds of yellow pollen. Unlike holly, hazel is monoecious, carrying both male and female flowers on the same tree; look at the twigs that have the catkins and you should find one or two tiny red tufts on the end of the thick green buds. These are the female flowers which will develop into cobnuts.

Borrowdale was once renowned for its nuts, but hazel bushes need a lot of light and the long period of neglect has resulted in a much reduced crop.

Keep to the wood edge until the track bears uphill to the left, to pick up the line of an old drystone wall. This leads past a National Trust sign to your left and through an old gateway. The track continues to bear left, leading out onto a grassy hillside.

To the north is a fine view of Castle Crag, a cone-shaped hill crying out for a castle. The nearest thing to a ruin today is actually the remains of a slate quarry, which did away with the original earthworks of a Romano-British or Iron Age settlement. The name Borrowdale comes from the Norse 'borgas dalr', the valley of the fortress, so it must once have been an impressive or memorable feature.

Take the grassy track slanting up to the left, following a ruined stone wall on the right. Where the wall ends a path leads downhill into a little wooded valley hiding Scaleclose Force. Do not take this but bear left and follow the wide grassy path as it meanders uphill to a wall. Continue with the wall on your left, to take a ladder stile to the left.

The wall has parsley fern growing in it, a plant which prefers high rocky places although it looks as if it ought to be in a herb garden. It does not smell like parsley at all and behaves like any other fern, producing spores rather than seeds.

The noise at this point is produced by Scaleclose Gill, a fast-flowing little torrent with its attractive waterfall hidden by the trees.

Go left uphill, contouring along a rather indistinct grassy path around the hillside for several hundred metres until a ladder stile can be seen to the right, in a stone wall.

To the left is a craggy knoll called High Doat. Jackdaws are usually in evidence, looking like small crows but delivering a noisy 'jack' instead of a 'caw'.

Jackdaws are a nuisance in some villages because of their habit of dropping sticks down chimneys. On crags like this it is easy to understand why they do it. There are no good nest sites in the vertical crevices, but if a stick can be lodged across a narrow gully a platform can be built-up by simply dropping more sticks on top of the first one. Deserted houses sometimes have their chimneys bunged up by thousands of sticks dropped by hundreds of persistent jackdaws; this does not seem to happen so much on open crags, presumably because even the most optimistic birds can see when it is not going to work.

To the north-west is High Scawdel, a shoulder of Dale Head which manages to obscure the main peak with impressive ease.

Bear right, towards the stile.

The dip in the ground should be crossed with care; it is a bog quite capable of wetting your ankles but containing some quite interesting plants, so if you have reasonable boots on it should be worth the inconvenience. The plant to look for is sundew, out in summer and autumn but very easy to overlook as it is usually quite tiny. It has round red-green leaves with sticky hairs which catch gnats and thereby provide the plant with essential nutrients. Sundew gained its name from the globules on the tips of the leaf-hairs, which look like dew but do not evaporate in the hot sunshine.

Gerard (of *Herbal* fame) wrote that 'cattle of the female kinde are stirred up to lust by eating even a small quantitie'. Check that there are no debauched cows about before you continue.

Cross the stile and turn left along the well-used track. Continue for several hundred metres.

Ahead and to the right is the road to Honister, snaking its way up a nasty incline which once had the R.S.P.C.A. campaigning against cruelty to pack horses. The route has changed somewhat and the original road is now no more than a green track, but the incline is as severe and modern cars complain a lot more than lowly horses ever did. Ahead and to the left is the Seathwaite fork of Borrowdale, famous for being the wettest inhabited place in England.

Under such circumstances one wonders why it continues to be inhabited; the annual rainfall is about 322cm.

The path ends with two adjacent gates. Go through the left one and take the wide grassy path downhill. At the stony track turn left and continue downhill to Seatoller.

Bridge at Longthwaite

51

Seatoller once had a manor, now reduced in status to a house but still a cut above the local cottages. There used to be a toll house too which is how some people think that the village got its name, but the Old Norse 'saetr' (summer pasture with the alder tree), is a more likely origin.

Yew Tree Cottage, on the right, is dated 1628, and has a yew tree outside it. Was there always a yew tree there, and, more particularly was it *that* yew tree? The answer is that it probably was not — the popular idea that yews grow to be hundreds or thousands of years old is a myth, propagated by people interpreting the Domesday Book too literally.

Continue to the car park.

You will probably find a cordon of chaffinches around your car; they seem to know when lunch is imminent.

Grange Fell

Walk Nine
GRANGE FELL

TROUTDALE — GRANGE FELL — WATENDLATH — HIGH LODORE; 7.5km

This route incorporates some of the best-known spots in northern Lakeland, yet it manages to do so within the context of a varied and exciting walk, using the woods, fells, falls and settlements as integral parts of a landscape rather than as snap-shot images.

Start at GR 262183. Park on the roadside close to the Borrowdale Hotel, 5km south of Keswick on the main road. Walk south on the right side of the main road for several hundred metres until the roadside path ends on a bend. Cross the road (carefully!) and turn up the gravelled track, signed 'Troutdale Cottages'.

The track is shadowed to the left and right by trees and bushes: copper beech, yew and laurel to the left, ash, hawthorn and elder to the right. Perhaps it is its sickly appearance and unpleasant smell that have given elder its dubious reputation. Evil is said to befall anyone who burns or cuts it down and tradition identifies it as the tree used by Judas for his suicide.

By contrast, enchanters' nightshade, which grows in the shade beneath the ash trees on the right, is a rather insignificant plant for such a portentous name, and has no particular magical associations.

A little further along the track is a very beautiful oak wood, growing on the steep north slope of Grange Crags.

At the end of the track is a five-bar gate.

Go through this and on for another 100m until a path bears left to meet a small stream.

The stream is called Comb Gill. About 50m from the main stream is a smaller tributary which runs through a series of narrow walled troughs, the remains of fish ponds built at a time when fresh trout was a welcome addition to the local diet.

The cropped grass on the banks of the stream is colonised by thyme and pignut as well as the usual trio of acid-grassland flowers — foxglove, tormentil and heath bedstraw. 'Bedstraw' was a name applied to any plant used to stuff a mattress in the days when it was prudent to replace the material regularly and get rid of the associated fleas.

After about 100m on the streamside bear right, away from the stream, uphill past a large boulder and through a birchwood.

The rock face to the south-east is Black Crag, containing one of the most famous of the Lake District climbing routes, Troutdale Pinnacles. It was first scaled by two local Borrowdale climbers, Mayson and Mallison, in 1914, at the end of a twenty-year golden age that had produced a generation of adventure-seekers. Those were the days when you shot your chums with a Thornton-Pickard folding ruby camera and crammed into the Wastwater Hotel to watch your heroes play billiard table fives. On the climb itself you were recommended to wear a Norfolk jacket fastened by bulldog buttons, and your footwear would have consisted of wet-day socks, shepherd's walking boots and clinkers.

Follow the path uphill, across a small side-stream and up towards a wall with, at its end by the main stream, a stile.

The craggy woodland was once the home of badgers, hence the name 'Brock Bield' on the map. The ground probably slopes too severely for oak to take a firm hold, so birch has remained the dominant tree. Birch is very short-lived, rarely surviving for more than a hundred years — by which time it has usually been superceded by other species. It is a pioneer of open ground and its seeds are unable to germinate in the shade of existing woodland, so in most situations its presence is a sign of previous clearance or the relief of grazing pressures.

53

Most mature birches are attacked by the polypore fungus, which sends out large hoof-shaped brackets from the trunk of any affected tree; these tough outgrowths were once used as razor strops, and the fine wood-dust caused by the decay was used by Swiss watch-makers as a polish. Apart from these obscure and obsolete uses foresters have afforded birch only one major virtue — that its sap makes a highly potent wine.

Go over the stile and up the steep path which bears away from the stream for a while.

The more enclosed canopy keeps the atmosphere damp and allows ferns to flourish. The humidity is also responsible for the surprising number of large black slugs (of a species called *Arion ater*), which seem to enjoy a crawl over the path.

Continue uphill to join a very stony path leading even more steeply up a wooded gully onto level open ground. About 100m further on is a fence and stile. Go over this and follow the narrow path up a heather-lined defile.

At the top, a detour of two or three metres on the left will bring you to a rocky knoll with a superb view of Keswick and Derwent Water. To the right (east) is Brown Dodd, to the left Cat Bells and Maiden Moor.

The path now descends towards a wall, at which bear right, keeping the wall to your left. Continue for several hundred metres; the path eventually leaves the wall and bears right, through heather.

Small heath butterfly

Down to the left is a rushy hollow called Long Moss. During the summer small heath butterflies will be on the wing here. They are tawny-brown in colour, and, like all the other members of the 'brown' (Satyrid) family of butterflies, have false eye-spots near the tip of the wings designed to frighten or distract birds. Years ago the large heath, a species characteristic of upland mires, probably occurred here as well, but it is now very rare in the Lake District. Most of the other classic mountain insects like the mountain ringlet butterfly and the orange-tailed bumblebee *Bombus monticola* are still found in this area, but there are few extensive 'mosses' left in Cumbria and the large heath has been unable to adapt to drier habitats.

Continue over the hill brow and join a substantial drystone wall. The path keeps to the right of this wall; after about 100m there is a ladder stile. Cross this and follow the grassy path which leads downhill, over a small stream, and towards a sheep pen.

The view to the right is of the narrow neck of Borrowdale, with Castle Crag (topped by a memorial cairn) the most eye-catching feature. Further south is the River Derwent and Johnny's Wood, with Base Brown and Great Gable in the distance.

The most notable insect of drier heath areas is the tiger beetle, a handsome bright-green creature which runs and flies at incredible speed and spends its life terrorising grubs and caterpillars. Like most predators it is unreliable in its habits, and is at its most active on sunny days. Each tiger beetle probably disposes of hundreds of 'pests' like the heather beetle and the anchor moth, but real heroes remain anonymous and there are no dialect poems dedicated to insects.

Walk past the sheep pen and up the short steep rise. At the top of the path is a junction. Turn sharp left and continue uphill through heather towards Brund Fell. The main path bears right between summit pinnacles.

A scramble of a few metres to the right will bring you to the top of Brund Fell, with an outstandingly craggy panorama typical of the volcanic rocks at the heart of the Lake District. The slabs and boulders bear scars from the Ice Age, lines etched by stones embedded in sheets of ice.

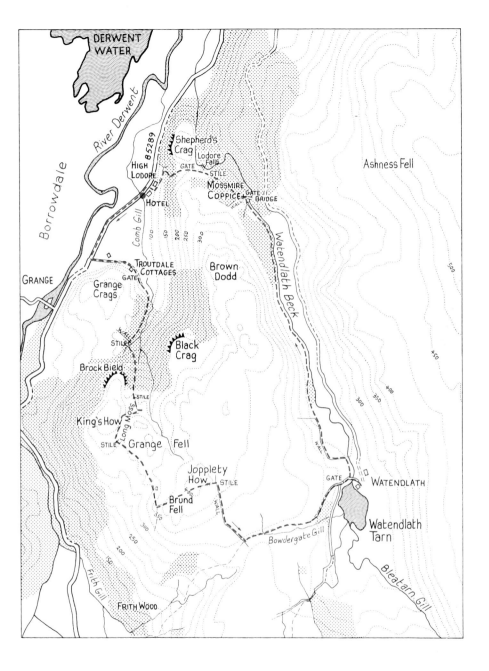

Back on the path, continue east-north-east over the craggy fell. Keep Jopplety How (a distinctive steep-sided hill) to the left and head downhill to a ladder stile over a wall. Cross the stile and turn right, following the wall downhill for several hundred metres.

To the left is some very marshy ground, so keep as close as possible to the wall. Swaledale sheep, identified by their black faces with white muzzles, inhabit the drier ground and are the commonest breed in the area. The world population of the other

55

characteristic breed, the Herdwick, probably stands at no more than 50,000, centred on Borrowdale where most tenancy agreements stipulate that the more traditional breed should be continued, but the Swaledale is considered more cost-effective and numbers have increased considerably in recent years.

Eventually a wide gravel track is reached, at which turn left. At first there is a fence to the right, but towards Watendlath this is replaced by a wall.

The view ahead and to the right is transformed by the appearance of Watendlath Tarn, either deep indigo or lead-grey depending on the state of the wind and weather. On the far side of the valley is a steep hillside incised here and there by tree-lined gullies, rising eastwards above Watendlath to the cairned summit of High Tove. Less than 2km the other side of this 515m hill top is Thirlmere, but because of the intervening spine of hills the distance by the road from here to the north shore of the reservoir is about 17km.

Follow the track down to Watendlath. Just before the packhorse bridge is a gate to the left.

This is the route to follow, but a short detour into the hamlet is hard to resist. The name 'Watendlath' has caused a great deal of speculation among would-be etymologists, culminating in the translation 'the barn at the end of the lake', with 'vatn' translated from Old Norse as the lake and 'endi' as the end. What 'lath' was is not so easily deduced, but the temptation to turn it into

View from Brund Fell summit — north-west clockwise to south

something appropriate has proved almost overwhelming.

Across from the bridge is a barn and a stable; to the right of this is Caffle House, a large whitewashed building offering refreshment to weary walkers. On the far right, flanking the southern side of the settlement, is a series of farm buildings lending the place an authentic flavour, vital to its credibility as the setting for much of Hugh Walpole's *Herries Chronicle*.

Go through the gate on the west bank of the stream. Follow the path for several hundred metres, first alongside the stream, then left at a wall and bearing right beneath the crags. Continue alongside the wall until the path bears right to bring you back to the stream, then keep close to its bank and continue north-north-west.

The water of Watendlath Beck provides a reliable source of insects for pied and grey wagtails, and for the common sandpiper and dipper. Wagtails have a special liking for gnats and other small winged creatures, and when the insect season is over they move downstream or, in the case of the pied wagtail, drift away to farmyards and fields to try a more varied diet. The sandpiper deserts the country entirely, spending the winter in southern Africa, leaving the dipper as the only regular inhabitant of the waterside during winter.

Keep to the path which eventually crosses a footbridge over a small sidestream, then enters a lightly-wooded area and leads to a stone wall with woodland behind and a footbridge to the right across Watendlath

Griisedale Pike Causey Pike Maiden Moor Cat Bells Skiddaw Bleaberry Fell High Seat Watendlath Val

Watendlath in December

Beck. **Do not cross the bridge but turn left. Continue for about 50m with the wall on your right until you reach a wicket gate. Go through this and walk down the woodland track.**

This is Mossmire Coppice, a block of sessile oak trees bedecked by mosses and lichens. Look closely at the trunks and you will probably find them alive with ants, not the little black creatures that suddenly appear in suburban kitchens but big red wood ants on patrol from their impressive nests on the forest floor. The ants coming down the trunks will have scoured the foliage in search of other insects and will be dragging their victims (often other ants) back to the nest to satisfy a million pairs of hungry mandibles.

If you find an anthill don't get too inquisitive. When ants get angry they squirt formic acid at any intruder, producing a shimmering blanket of gas which quickly brings

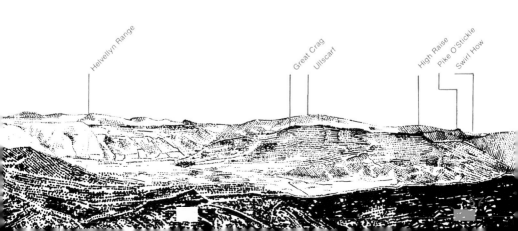

tears to the eyes. Green woodpeckers, which inhabit this wood and feed almost exclusively on ants when they are in season, deliberately wade-in among their prey allowing the formic acid to fumigate their plumage.

Continue along the track for about 200m, to a rocky gap with wooded slopes to left and right. Just as the track starts to descend towards a stream, take a path which bears left. Go over a stile and bear left again. A little further on is a wicket gate.

To the right are the famous Lodore Falls, partly obscured in the summer because of the undergrowth, but this seems only to enhance the mystery of the place. In 1829 Parson and White's Directory observed that on the nearby crag 'oak ash birch holly and wild rose, hang in wanton luxuriance'. So they still do, but the accompanying description of Lodore as the 'Niagara of England' was taking enthusiasm a little too far.

The damp atmosphere of the gorge encourages ferns and mosses to grow in particular abundance, earning it a mention in many botanic text books. It is also of interest to geologists, forming a shelf between the Borrowdale Volcanic Series of rocks and the Skiddaw Series. But most of all Lodore attracts attention because it is noisy, bustling and beautiful.

About 50m further on, close to a small side-stream by a clump of young birch trees, the path forks; bear left, continue on through a gap in an old wall, then follow the obvious path which zig-zags downhill into Borrowdale, through open woodland to emerge by a stone wall. Go left, through High Lodore Farm to the main road and the Borrowdale Hotel.

Stonethwaite Valley, with Eagle Crag in the distance

Walk Ten
DOCK TARN &
WATENDLATH

ROSTHWAITE — WILLYGRASS GILL — DOCK TARN — WATENDLATH; 7.5km

A very varied walk, starting along the Stonethwaite Beck but ascending suddenly and steeply through woodland to exposed fell, with notable tarns and a few mires along the way. As with most routes that include open fell landscapes, keep this for a reasonably clear day.

Park at the Keswick (north) end of Rosthwaite, on the east side of the road at GR 258149, or at the car park just up the track opposite the Post Office (the end house). Take the metalled track going east on the Keswick side of the Post Office, signposted 'Hazel Bank Hotel'. This leads to a bridge.

It is remarkable how level the bed of the beck is, and how vividly the blue-green stones shine through the water. The structure of a watercourse is a product of several factors, of which the velocity of the current is the most important. At anything more than a metre per second the flow is described as 'torrential' and there is no chance of any silt or sand settling to provide an anchorage for aquatic plants. Occasional 'spates' or flash-floods dislodge or shuffle even the largest stones, settling them again to form a regular, level bed. Apart from the fish, most aquatic animal life is found under the stones; creatures like mayfly nymphs and freshwater shrimps emerge from their shelter at night when they are not so likely to be eaten by wagtails and water shrews.

Cross the bridge and take the right turn before Hazel Bank Hotel.

Hugh Walpole had this house in mind when he wrote *Rogue Herries* — the first book in the long Herries saga. The house is reminiscent of the novels: solid and reliable.

Walk along the walled track with the river on your right.

The bushes on the right are hazel and bird cherry; neither achieves great stature but they are attractive in their season and thoroughly British.

Across the beck is the back of Rosthwaite, and with one notable exception the rear view is just as interesting as the front. The houses are very square, the windows small and functional. Compare the walls and roofs of neighbouring dwellings; thick irregular slates are the genuine article, but even they do not last forever and have had to be replaced in some cases.

Continue along the track.

After the village the most obvious features are the high walls. To the left are some narrow fields, old enclosures used as pasture but without any shelter for stock, so the walls serve a dual function. Most of the drystone walls in the Lake District are the result of 18th or 19th century enclosure awards, but some go back much further — perhaps a thousand years — when flat valley land was cleared around key communities. These settlements bear the suffix 'thwaite', an indication that they date back to the times of Norse settlers arriving from Ireland in the 10th century. Rosthwaite was 'the clearing marked by, or surrounding, a cairn'.

Across the river valley to the right (south-west) is the other fork of Borrowdale, leading away to Seathwaite. Johnny's Wood (see page 48) lies in the foreground.

Follow the track, alternately closely walled or across open fields, for several hundred metres until another track (from Stonethwaite) joins it from the right.

Stonethwaite is another ancient settlement, this time requiring no translation — the name probably records the sheer frustration of trying to clear a few acres of ground in what still seems to be the pebbliest place in

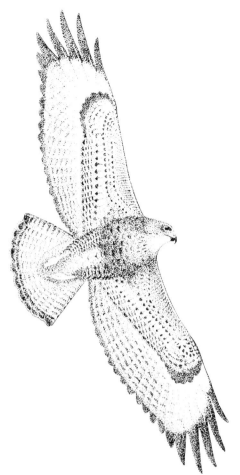

Buzzard

tracks merge) and turn left, signposted 'footpath to Dock Tarn'. The path leads up-hill through open woodland, then climbs more steeply to a stile in a wall, finally zig-zagging very steeply indeed through rather dense woodland.

There are several features of interest if an excuse is needed to rest, such as Willygrass Gill, noisy but pretty, with its attractive little gorge to the right of the stile.

The trees are sessile or Durmast oaks, and although they are the natural tree cover for acidic soils on western hillsides they were probably planted as an economic crop, either to replace existing tree cover or poor quality sheep walk. The only good reason for not extending rough grazing over all the common land during the 18th and 19th centuries was if a better return could be secured from woodland industries. The major occupations involved were bark-stripping to produce tannin for leather manufacture, and charcoal-burning to produce fuel for smelting.

The only clues left today are the trees themselves — they often have two or three stems instead of a single trunk, a sign that they were once coppiced (i.e. cut off just above the ground) to force the growth of additional shoots.

At the top of the wood follow the cairned path, easier now, past a small stone structure used as a sheep fold.

This is a good place to stop and look over the valley; the quick ascent through the wood makes it possible to appreciate the contrast in both landscape and land use. These upper fells have always been remote from the farms below, especially in winter.

Prior to the Agrarian Revolution, a percent-age of each man's flock of sheep had to be killed every year because of insufficient grazing. Life among the farmers and shepherds was very frugal in such isolated valleys, and there are several contemporary accounts of unmitigated squallor. It says much for romantic duplicity that Gilpin, writing in 1772, saw things rather differ-ently:

Their herds afford them milk; and their flocks, cloaths . . . the sheep and shep-herds are clothed alike; both in the simple livary of nature.

Cumbria. Across the valley is Bull Crag, topped by Hanging Haystack, a good place to look out for buzzards which like to soar above the wooded crags in search of rabbits or carrion. They are the most likely birds of prey to be seen in the area, though there are also sparrowhawks, peregrines and kestrels.

Continue south-east, through a gate and as before, with the wall to your right.

An alternative to the stony track is to walk along a parallel grassy path a few metres up the hillside. The wood to the left is of oak but the more open lower slopes also contain a few ash and holly trees, both en-couraged by farmers who once used them as fodder.

Go through the next gate (where all the

60

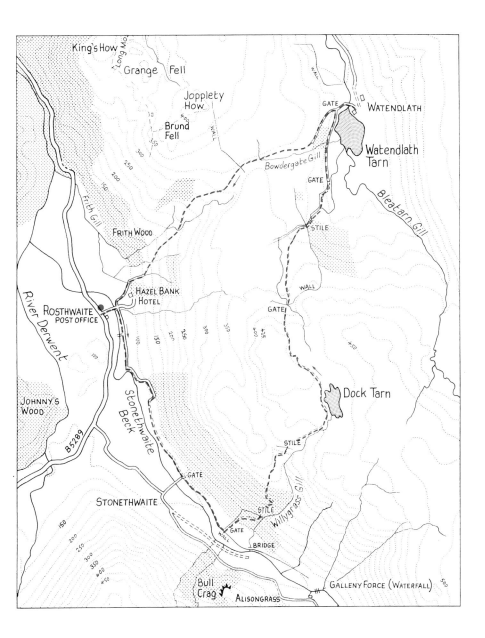

Tenant and yeoman farmer alike rejoiced at the arrival of the turnip at the end of the 18th century. Henceforth there was no need for any return to autumn slaughter and smoked carcasses ceased to clutter cottage firesides.

The view south is dominated by Eagle Crag with Greenup Edge on the opposite (eastern) side of Greenup Gill. Three kilometres beyond Eagle Crag is High Raise with, two kilometres further in the distance, the Langdale Pikes.

61

Continue around the head of a little valley and over a stile.

There is an impressive view to the right, a fine sweep to Greenup Gill and its headwater towards High Raise.

The path makes its way through some sturdy heather, a plant which needs to be burnt or cut down every few years to encourage fresh growth, and which often suffers from overgrazing.

Follow a path alongside a stream to Dock Tarn.

The tarn probably got its name from the Old English 'docce', meaning a water lily or other aquatic plant. High altitude tarns like this are often very acidic and few water plants do well, except those specifically adapted to them such as the curious little awlwort. The same is true for most birds, though the common sandpiper, known locally as the 'willylilt', is a regular visitor during the spring.

Take the path along the nearside (i.e. west bank) of the tarn, past a knoll to the left. The path continues north-west with a boggy area to the right.

Cumbrians have almost as many names for bogs as Eskimos do for snow. This one probably qualifies as a 'flother', a rather wet type with sphagnum moss and bog cotton. The little islands, protected from sheep, have clusters of bog asphodel — one of the loveliest of upland plants, producing bright yellow flowers in August.

Follow the path north, descending to a gate in a wall.

In the distance Watendlath Tarn and its adjacent green fields catch the eye like an oasis in a wilderness. The wide sweep of marshy ground ahead is colonised by a classic plant community composed of bog myrtle and purple moor grass. Bog myrtle is an unattractive name for a low straggly shrub with few outstanding features, but the crushed leaves give off a gloriously appetising smell. Before the introduction of hops it was used to flavour beer, providing the brew with enough body 'to make a man quickly drunke', according to Gerard's *Herbal*.

◁ *Watendlath Beck and Tarn*

Purple moor grass is also rather inconspicuous for most of the year, producing a tall, rather sparse head of purple-brown seeds. But during the late summer and autumn the old stems turn a warm orange, bringing an unexpected change of colour to the wetlands and fells. The leaves curl back and break off in the autumn winds, earning the plant its country name of 'flying bent'.

For about 200m the path is quite clear, but then it fades and is difficult to make out. Keep on the same line, however, heading slightly to the right with Skiddaw on the skyline. After a few hundred metres of gentle descent the various small paths join together, then bear right to follow a wall to a ladder stile where four enclosure walls meet. Go over the stile and follow the clear path by a stream and stone wall down to an enclosed lane. Go through the gate.

To the right (east) is the lightly wooded scarp slope above Bleatarn Gill, which feeds into Watendlath Tarn. The gnarled trees by the track are ash pollards, their branches cut back so that they often seem half-dead. The twigs of the ash are thick and brittle, tipped for most of the year by sooty black buds. An Anglo-Saxon cure for deafness ran as follows: 'take a green stick of ash, lay it over a fire, take the juice that comes out, put it in wool, and stick it in the ear'. A desperate remedy!

Continue along the track towards Watendlath. Just before the wicket gate on the edge of the hamlet is a path leading obliquely to the left, signposted to Rosthwaite. This is the route to follow, but a short detour into Watendlath will add little to the total length of the walk.

There is also a little tea room, not to be dismissed lightly. Watendlath Tarn is charming, circled by a ring of water lilies and stocked with trout — less like an upland tarn than a large village pond.

Before the Dissolution of the Monasteries this area was owned by the Cistercians of Fountains Abbey in Yorkshire, who fished the waters and tended their flocks in splendid isolation, for this is a curiously lonely place even on a sunny day when tourists are everywhere.

From the Rosthwaite turn walk uphill, heading south-west.

After several hundred metres the ground levels over a wide hill brow, with Jopplety How and Grange Fell high to the right. Alongside the track runs a line of telegraph poles, not pretty but important to the local community. Many features of modern civilisation are obtrusive in the countryside and none more so than power cables and telegraph wires. The Friends of the Lake District waged a successful battle in 1937 to prevent electricity pylons invading the area and most power lines now run underground, but the cost prohibits a total cover-up.

Follow the track, stony in places, as it winds downhill through light woodland. Just before a small stream (Frith Gill) turn right through a gap in the wall, descending again to rejoin the stream a little further down. Cross it via a raised walkway, continue past Hazel Bank Hotel and turn right, back to Rosthwaite.

A wall stile

Walk Eleven
STONETHWAITE

STONETHWAITE — GALLENY FORCE — JOHNNY HOUSE — ALISONGRASS; 4km

A short walk over level ground, often stony and difficult during very wet weather when the fells can brood ominously on all sides, yet remarkable for the ease with which quiet rurality gives way to apparent wilderness, and for the constantly changing character of Stonethwaite Beck.

Start from GR 263137. Park in Stonethwaite village, close to the telephone kiosk if this is possible. From this kiosk take the track leading towards the beck.

Close to the cottages the track is overhung with wild cherry.

A notice on the bridge states that it was erected in 1899 but had to be rebuilt in 1979. Being swept away or damaged by torrential spates of water is the normal fate for most bridges in Cumbria, and accounts for the relative scarcity of picturesque stone structures.

From the bridge the whole valley seems to be heavily wooded, especially downstream where the Borrowdale oakwoods cover most of the lower slopes. 'Thwaite' means a clearing however, and there is little doubt that early settlers found a terrace here from where they could begin to push back the wildwood and create pasture for their stock.

Go over the bridge and through a gate to the junction with another track. Turn right.

The deformed trees are ash. Cutting off the branches at head-height is a process known as pollarding, a traditional form of management designed to provide a self-renewing crop every few years. It used to provide farmers with a dual harvest, the wood being sent away to make tool handles whilst the foliage and bark were fed to stock. Unfortunately cheap imports of hickory from the New World killed off the market for ash wood, and it was discovered that dairy cattle produced poorer milk yields when fed on ash leaves.

Pollarding may produce deformed trees but for some reason it increases their life expectancy, and most of Britain's oldest trees were pollarded at some time in their youth.

Follow the trackway up the valley, keeping the wall to your right.

A very stony track; the larger boulders to the left have been colonised by interesting plants such as foxglove and parsley fern, contrasting with the wall itself which is in heavy shade and has little growing on it except a few lichens.

The open ground between the track and the oakwood is grazed by sheep, and there is a small circular fold or pen used by shepherds to hold flocks temporarily or to provide shelter for ewes with lambs.

After a few hundred metres the wood on the left begins to recede and, after passing a small larch plantation, the path leads over a small bridge across Willygrass Gill.

Pollarded tree

65

The view to the right is of Bull Crag, a steep wooded slope with an attractive jumble of rocks. Large black birds will probably be crows, but *very* large black birds might be ravens. They keep to the upper crags above the tree line and are usually seen either singly or in pairs. Considering their size and bulk, ravens are masters of flight and will often perform acrobatic tumbles and twists for the sheer pleasure of it. They are still common in the Lake District, despite persecution and a bad reputation. The Ancient Greeks thought that rubbing a raven's egg into your hair prevented it from going grey, but apparently there was a risk that the magic might be too powerful and turn your teeth black.

Continue along the track for another few hundred metres to pass a group of yew trees and a small stone ruin.

Yews are often associated with habitation, and particularly with churchyards. In pagan times the tree held great spiritual significance and was planted in sacred places, so when Christianity took over the sacred places it also took over the yew. When a venerable old tree died it was replaced with a new one, and so on down the years.

This group of yews has examples of both sexes, the male developing little green or yellow flowers in the summer and the female producing bright red arils in autumn. The aril contains a clear sticky goo enclosing the seed, and for some reason thrushes find this irresistible.

Keep to the same track. After a slight rise in level it descends again to lead through a gate.

The track is very stony and is in the process of being eroded away by the beck. The channel fills very rapidly after rain; this is because it is fed by many small streams or gills taking run-off from the immediate

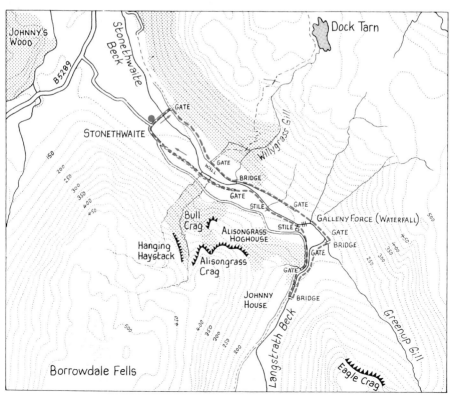

Yew trees and sheep fold, Stonethwaite Beck in the distance

fells rather than from distant headstreams. The small waterfall, called Galleny Force, is best viewed from the other bank on the return leg, but is still worth a look.

A little way ahead is a sheep-fold. Take the wicket gate to the right just before this is reached, leading to a footbridge over Greenup Gill.

Looking at the bare stones and the fierce current it is difficult to believe that anything can live in the water, but several insects have adapted themselves to the conditions and are to be found clinging to the undersides of submerged stones. The most dramatic are the larvae of mayflies and stoneflies, which have incredibly flattened bodies and long tails. They are full-grown in the spring, just before they change into adults, but are very nimble and difficult to catch. Along with caddisfly larvae they are the chief food-source for the trout and for riverside birds like the dipper.

Go over the bridge and through a wicket gate.

To the left is one of the most desolate valleys in the whole area, guarded by Eagle Crag, which lost its eyrie many years ago. Eagles were never popular with farmers: 'The devastation made on the fold, in the breeding season, by one eyrie is computed as a lamb a day' wrote Father West in the 18th century. He also described how this site was destroyed by a shepherd 'let down the summit of this dreadful rock by a rope of twenty fathoms'. The rope referred to was paid for by general subscription, and was kept in Borrowdale for this express purpose. No doubt the eagles tried to rebuild again and again for they are remarkably faithful to traditional sites, but in the end they went the way of all predators.

Walk alongside the Langstrath Beck for a little way before bearing left to pick up the path.

This gives you the opportunity to explore a beautifully sculpted little chasm through which the beck runs. There are cascades of white water and deep pools refracting the green or turquoise of submerged boulders. The colour comes from chlorite contained in the volcanic rocks.

Walk south-west along the grassy path, marshy in places, through a gap in a ruined drystone wall, to a footbridge over Langstrath Beck.

A substantial bridge which seems out of proportion to the amount of traffic it carries. Presumably anything less robust would be washed away when Langstrath Beck asserted itself. The banks are overhung by some fine downy birches, their trunks less white than silver birch and their young twigs slightly pubescent. There are also some rowans, which produce lovely orange berries popular with wine-makers.

To the left the dale of Langstrath leads away to Esk Hause, the wettest place in England. Langstrath is one of the least spoiled and least visited of the main valleys,

just as desolate as the route alongside Greenup Gill and reaching much further into the core of the Lake District.

The surrounding fells are reputed to 'attract the vapours', and there is often a soggy blanket of cloud hanging over the dale head.

Go over the footbridge and turn right. Follow the track to a gate.

There is an old oak tree to the right. Oak produces its foliage quite late into the spring, usually just after the ash. The rhyme 'ash before oak and we're in for a soak' is therefore a safe enough prediction in most years. Another weather-inspired verse, 'If the thrush sings 'fore Candlemas Day it does nowt after but repent and pray' is a saying based on a much better appreciation of Lake District weather. Candlemas is February 2nd, and thrushes have a nasty habit of starting too early after a mild winter.

By the middle of the summer oak leaves are usually peppered with holes, having been the food for a vast array of caterpillars,

Stonethwaite village

Yarrow

bugs and beetles. More species of insects feed on oak than on any other tree, and from the end of June the foliage begins to bear the scars. It is not an unequal contest, however, for the oak produces tannins which gradually make the leaves inedible. Insects therefore have to time their breeding season to coincide with the period of early leaf growth.

Keep to the track, which veers left away from the beck only to rejoin it after 200m. A track then bears left, towards a small building, but avoid this and instead go over a stile to keep close to the beck.

Upstream the beck is at its most beautiful, not to be passed without stopping for at least a moment's contemplation.

The little hut to the left is a 'hogg house', built not to accommodate pigs (which were known as 'gris'), but young sheep or 'hoggs'. The normal practice in the 18th and 19th centuries was to keep the replacement stock in these buildings during the worst of the winter and feed them on hay. When the young sheep were into their third year they were introduced into the flock, by which time they were robust and healthy enough to survive and bear lambs.

Continue along the path; the ground rises slightly to a ladder stile, after which it levels out to a wide grassy shelf.

This is an area popular with campers. As well as the usual yarrow and foxglove there is a healthy population of plantain, a low-growing plant appearing wherever man upsets the normal vegetation. Red Indians called it 'white man's footprint' and Nature Reserve wardens find it in all sorts of unwanted places, and probably call it something worse.

Carry on north-west towards Stonethwaite.

Quite suddenly you are entering an agricultural landscape of level pastures and ash pollards. This area can have changed little since the 13th century, when it formed part of the thriving vaccary (dairy farm) of Stonethwaite. It was so desirable a property that the abbeys of Furness and Fountains squabbled for years over ownership, until Edward I was obliged to confiscate it. This was in 1304; the Abbot at Fountains must have been a shrewd businessman for he immediately offered the King 40 shillings and got the place back without any redress from Furness.

Go through a gate and along the road back to the car park.

Look at the gardens as you go by, phlox and magnolia, Victorian to the core. The walls of the cottages are whitewashed, layer upon layer of the stuff, until after a few centuries the surface has grown to resemble thick icing. Byres and outbuildings were not painted — air whistling through gaps in the walls kept cattle free from T.B., and hay cool enough to prevent fermentation or spontaneous combustion.

Continue along the road to the car park.

69

Walk Twelve
BUTTERMERE

A CIRCUIT OF THE LAKE; 7km

A walk of reflected glory, the fells mirrored in a sheet of glass. Buttermere is one of the few lakes with a footpath right around it. The steep fells on either side, wooded on the lower slopes but dramatically un-tamed, contrast with the level past-ures to the north-east and south-west and the smooth surface of the water. The 'Buttermere Round' was one of the most popular Victorian walks; they eulogised it in a way that would seem excessive even by modern holiday brochure standards, yet much of the praise was well-merited. It is varied, easy underfoot, and suitable for all ages.

Start at GR 174169. Park in the village car park close to the Fish Hotel. Facing the hotel bear left, following a wide track sign-posted as 'public bridleway to Buttermere'.

The Fish Hotel figures in a famous story. Mary Robertson, who lived at what was then the Fish Inn, fell in love with a dashing gentleman calling himself the Honourable Alexander Augustus Hope. He had arrived in Keswick in July 1802 and the country girl of 18 was so infatuated that by October they were married. Doubts among the local gentry resulted in a series of sensational revelations; the man turned out to be John Hatfield who had left two wives and a pile of debts behind him. He was hanged for forgery in September 1803 leaving Mary alone and with child. The story of the Keswick Imposter and the Buttermere Beauty became the subject of many a soulful ballad, displaying little respect for poor Mary Robertson who had to live on in the village, older but wiser.

The track soon turns left. At the gate go over the stile on the left and continue along the main track as it bears right.

The hedges may not look very ancient but they have probably been here for several hundred years. Their age can be estimated by counting the different species of trees or bushes along a 30m section, each species adding a hundred years to the total. Within a few metres of this gate there are hawthorn, ash, hazel, elder, dog rose and sloe, suggesting that these hedges might have been here as field boundaries when Buttermere first got its name (translated as 'mere surrounded by good grazing land').

Walk along the track to a footbridge; go over this and bear left.

Just across the bridge is a birch tree bear-ing curious bunches of twigs looking rather like displaced crows' nests. They are called witches' brooms for obvious reasons, but the magic involved has more to do with chemicals than sorcery; fungi and/or bacteria attack the branches which respond by throwing out a chaotic tangle of buds and twigs.

Cross Sourmilk Gill, and make for the gate across the rough boulders.

Sourmilk Gill, which cascades down from Bleaberry Tarn, divides Scales Wood from Burtness. The latter is dominated by larch. Nobody really knows when larch was introduced into Britain, but it was certainly here in the early 17th century. By 1800 it had become a plantation tree and the subject of a long-standing argument about the wisdom of sacrificing tradition to rapid profit. Today even larch is considered to be too slow-growing to be of great economic value, and the current craze is for spruce.

Continue along the lakeside track, with the woods to your right.

The open canopy of larch and birch lets in a good deal of light, so there is plenty of vegetation on the woodland floor. Compare this with the dour spruce plantation a kilometre further along the track.

◁ *Fleetwith Pike, from the north-west shore of Buttermere*

71

This section of Burtness Wood is good for fungi in the late autumn. The most common toadstools are *Russula* and *Boletus*. *Russulas* usually have watery-purple or red caps with white stem and gills, whilst *Boletus* species are easy to recognise because they have tiny pores rather than gills, giving the underside a sponge-like appearance. *Boletus* are very chunky solid-looking toadstools, and have incredibly thick stems designed to hold the cap rigid and let the spores drop straight out.

The track goes through a gateway in an old drystone wall and into a much less varied section of woodland. Continue south-east until the wood ends at a gate and you are out on the open fell.

There is a good view across Buttermere to the left. The water is very clear, often with a slight turquoise cast produced by slate dust washed down from Honister Quarry by Gatesgarthdale Beck. It is a very infertile lake, second only to Wastwater in its lack of nutrients and therefore its shortage of aquatic plants, but it contains the char — a rare salmon-like fish once prized as being 'more luscious and delicious than the trout'. Char are only found in deep lakes, and Buttermere at 29m probably only just qualifies.

Behind the lake are the craggy fells astride Hassnesshow Beck. This area was once known as the last breeding site for golden eagles in the Lake District. Eagles eat young lambs and their presence in sheep country has always caused hostility among farmers. Add to this a good helping of persecution by gamekeepers and it is hardly surprising that they disappeared over a century ago. The long-awaited return to Cumbria came in 1969; since then they have nested successfully a few miles away and a pair may yet come back to these crags.

Walk along the path to cross Comb Beck to the right of a small larch wood.

The steep fell to the right is very impressive, the peaks of High Stile and High Crag linked by Comb Crags and the ice-sculpted bowl of Burtness Comb. This area holds another interesting animal story, because forty years ago a strange creature was discovered high up on Burtness Comb. It was brought down to Gatesgarth Farm and became a family pet, looked after by the farmer's daughter who had a way with animals and already had several foxes about the place. The mysterious animal turned out to be a pine marten, and it is strange that none of the local people recognised it: martens were once widespread in the district.

Pine martens were called 'sweet marts' to distinguish them from evil smelling 'foul marts' or polecats, which were known to have a liking for chickens and were quickly exterminated. But the pine martens did little harm and were far more elusive.

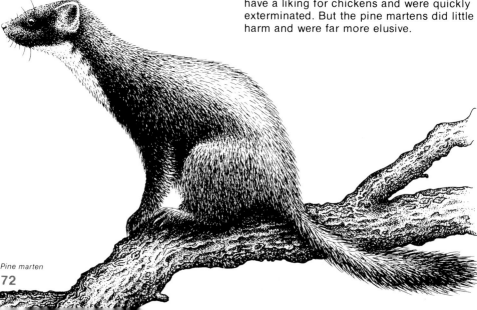

Pine marten

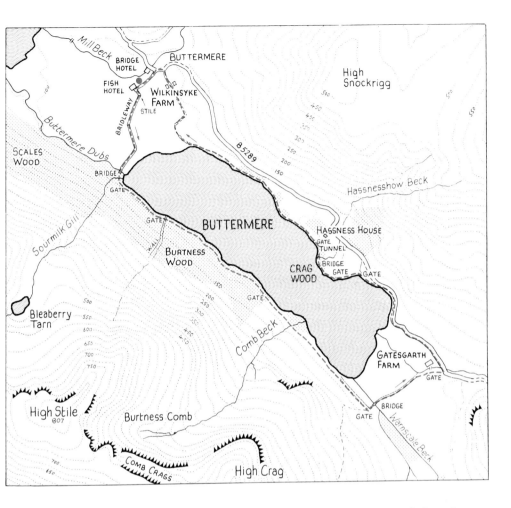

Perhaps they still inhabit the high woods and fells of Ennerdale; certainly they still survive in Grizedale Forest and are known to be great wanderers.

Eventually the path runs alongside a wall.

Ahead are Gatesgarthdale and Warnscale, two deep valleys gouged out a million years ago by glaciers converging from Honister and Great Gable. They met at Fleetwith Pike, and when the ice melted all that remained of the underlying rock was the sharp ridge of Fleetwith Edge. Little pieces of the Lake District were carried all over northern England, to be dumped as far south as the Cheshire Plain.

Turn left just after a sheep-fold, towards a gate. Go through the gate and along the straight track, over Warnscale Beck and on to Gatesgarth Farm.

Originally there were three farms, each with its own flock of Herdwick sheep. Gatesgarth is the only one still functioning; it maintains a genuine tradition in a place otherwise dedicated to tourism, and there are often interesting activities in progress. Observe from a distance and try not to get in the way. The busiest time is probably September and October when the autumn sales are in progress and the holding pens are full.

Sheep carry two identification features to establish ownership. The most obvious is the smit-mark on the fleece, usually red and derived originally from local haematite. The second is the lug-mark, a hole clipped in the ear to provide permanent proof of origin.

At the main road turn left, go over the bridge and continue for several hundred metres until the open shore is reached. At the small parking area take the path along the lakeside, signposted 'Buttermere via lakeshore path'.

This is the best part of the lake for fly fishing. Buttermere has an unusually wide assortment of fish species, but they are rarely found in the same section of water; trout prefer the shallows whilst pike and perch are most common close to the north-east shore where the edge shelves steeply.

Follow the path around the rocky eastern lake shore, through a wicket gate across a field, through another wicket gate and towards the pine trees of Crag Wood.

Interesting to compare the Scots pine growing in a gap close to the shore with those on the edge of the field a little to the north-east. Those growing in the group are tall and straight with few lower branches and a characteristic platform of foliage at the top. This is what we expect pine trees to look like, but they only grow like this because they have to compete for light. Look at the ones at the wood edge, more rounded with hefty boughs and a lot more greenery. Beautiful trees, native north of the Border but introduced here many hundreds of years ago.

Go on a few more metres towards a foot-bridge.

Pines were not the only trees to be re-distributed around Britain in the dim and distant past. There are some attractive beech trees here, this time brought up from the south of England.

The tunnel on the shoreline path around Buttermere

Buttermere, from the north-west

The ground beneath the trees is usually littered with the opened husks of beech nuts, known as mast. Mice and squirrels seem to prefer acorns if they have the choice, and in any case the mast crop is unreliable and bonanza years are infrequent.

Cross the footbridge; the path now follows a much rockier course around the lake shore, and through a short tunnel.

The tunnel was built in the last century at the instigation of George Benson who owned Hassness House. He wanted to keep his men busy during the winter and must have been pleased with the result. An idle fancy to while away the idle moments; whether his men followed the same reasoning is another matter.

Go through a wicket gate and through some attractive parkland of lime, beech and sycamore. At the end of the lake continue straight ahead and then bear right, over a rocky piece of ground.

The gain in height offers a good view of the flat alluvial land that links Buttermere to Crummock Water. The lakes were once joined, and the flat deposits of silt and pebbles hardly seem enough to keep them apart.

Follow the waymarked track, through Wilkinsyke Farm and on to the village.

Wilkinsyke, one of the 17th century farms at the core of the Buttermere community, is a gem, especially for those who believe in the dog and stick image of agriculture. The path goes right through the yard, so take care not to put your foot in anything.

If you have time, look round the village and try to sort out which are the really old buildings; most of them have an interesting story to tell, though few inhabitants apart from Mary Robertson have gained fame or notoriety. A minor exception is John Norman, who lived in the terrace of white cottages at the northern end of the village and had the misfortune to be on HMS *Bounty* with Captain Bligh.

Walk Thirteen
HAY STACKS

GATESGARTH — SCARTH GAP — HAY STACKS — GREEN CRAG — WARNSCALE BECK; 7.5km

The most difficult walk in this book, involving a long climb up Scarth Gap and some rock-hopping in high country. The beauty and variety of scenery make it irresistible however, and many fell connoisseurs such as Wainwright hold it very close to their hearts, only lamenting that it is not a little higher. Save it for a clear day; any mist will not only obscure views but may also make parts of the route dangerous.

Park at the National Park car park at the southern end of Buttermere, on the Honister road opposite Gatesgarth Farm, GR 196150. Cross the road and go through the wicket gate just before the bridge, signposted 'public footpath to Scarth Gap'.

To the right is Gatesgarthdale Beck which draws its water from Honister. A local legend tells of a time in the 14th century when the beck ran red following a skirmish between Freebooters and English Borderers. The Freebooters, rustlers of the Graeme clan who had crossed the border to steal cattle, laid a trap between Honister and Yew Crags; the English Borderers, marching from Borrowdale, walked straight into it. The result was bloody and brief and both chiefs were killed.

Across the sycamore-lined beck is Gatesgarth Farm — though its byres and buildings are on this side, to the left of the path. There were once two other farms in the vicinity and a chapel on the roadside opposite Gatesgarth Cottage, but the community dwindled and has lost any individual identity.

After the farmyard bear left to go through a wicket gate and along a track with a wall and fence to the right.

To the left across the pasture is Low Raven Crag, rising sharply on a knife-edged ridge or 'arête' to Fleetwith Pike. On the lower slopes to the left is a small white cross, placed as a monument to Fanny Mercer, a girl killed in an accident in 1887.

Continue along the track towards a bridge.

The green pasture has been used as in-bye for sheep grazing for hundreds of years, always stocked with Herdwick sheep. Nobody knows how the breed originated; there is a story that a ship from the Spanish Armada was wrecked on the coast and forty sheep were rescued. Recent genetic investigation has shown some affinities with Scandinavian breeds so it seems more likely that the Herdwick's ancestors were introduced by Norse settlers, probably in the 10th century.

The name Herdwick or 'Herdwyck' is derived not from the actual name of the breed but from the traditional habit of leasing a farm to a tenant with a 'herd' of sheep. In hill country it is not practicable to take a flock from one farm to another because sheep take a long time to get to know the best grazing and shelter, so the flock is 'heafted', considered part and parcel of the farm.

Cross the bridge and continue along the track to a gate.

The view all around is of a glaciated landscape, especially the basin of Warnscale to the left which was hollowed-out by hundreds of metres of ice. Warnscale Beck is little more than a silver thread lost in an amphitheatre, though it is the focal point of the dale head. Ahead and to the right are the buttressed peaks of High Crag and High Stile with, between them, a classic 'cirque' (or cwm or corrie) called Burtness Comb, which held its core of ice high above the main valley now occupied by Buttermere. The reason the fells on the south-west side of the valley are so craggy is that the rocks of their upper slopes, being of the Borrow-

◁ *Autumn at Gatesgarth Farm; a pen full of Herdwick sheep*

77

dale Volcanic Series, have not weathered as easily as the older Skiddaw Slates, on which Buttermere actually sits.

Go through the gate and up the rather stony path which zig-zags steeply before finally bearing sharp left on a long but gradual ascent heading for Scarth Gap.

A little way after the turn is a wicket gate, a convenient place to look out over Warnscale Bottom to the left. The dominant feature is the marshy lower reach of the beck and its outfall with the grey stony shore of Buttermere. The green pasture-land ends abruptly to the south-east and it is possible to make out several drainage channels cut through the tussocky, rush-covered marshland to divert flood water away from the fields. During very wet weather this whole piece of land can disappear under a sheet of water, and the high water-table has obviously killed many of the pine trees on this side of the beck.

On the far side of the valley is Fleetwith Edge rising to the 648m (2,126ft) peak of Fleetwith Pike. The track arcing around its foot is the return route.

The path takes the easiest line obliquely up the hillside, making for the gap between two rocky crags.

The upper one of these is High Wax Knott, the clefts of its face lightly covered with heather and some small bushes of holly and rowan. This is a good place to look

Alpine lady's mantle

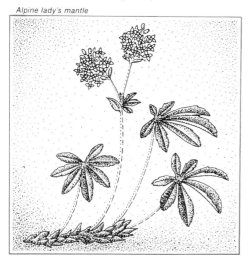

ahead to the Hay Stacks massif which can look remarkably doomy if the weather has turned bad. If a heavy mist has crept over Big Stack (the outer tooth) then it is time to think seriously of retreating the way you have come. Thick mist is the bane of any walker, though William Gilpin once wrote a piece entitled *The Beauty of Fog* in which he noted that 'among the beautiful appearances of fogs and mists, their gradual going off may be observed'. This is an aesthetic exercise you may wish to be spared.

The path contours to a gap in an old enclosure wall, then ascends Scarth Gap Pass, following the cairns.

Around the rocks and boulders are several flowers, among them a true mountain species called alpine lady's mantle. It has obscure yellow flowers but the leaves are distinctive, multi-fingered and resembling a miniature laburnum. Sheep graze most of the exposed patches but there are some better clumps hidden in the higher clefts.

Continue for about 200m over the flat brow of Scarth Gap. This leads towards a line of posts.

The posts are an old boundary, separating Ennerdale from the wilds beyond. To the right is the tip of Ennerdale Forest, a dark and sad place full of regimented conifers.

Just before the posts, bear left to follow a path which gains height very gradually for about 150m then, at a small cairn, turn sharp left up a steep and stony scramble marked by cairns to a grassy shelf or promontory, at which bear left.

A really excellent view soon opens up to the north-west, over Buttermere and Crummock Water and, if the day is very clear, to the Solway Firth and the Scottish hills.

Bear right, spiralling up to an iron post.

The view is now of the south face of Fleetwith Pike. It is remarkable how in very good visibility distance is foreshortened and deceptive, but the sheep-fold at the foot of the bracken-covered slope gives some idea of scale.

The path bears left of the next iron post, then left and uphill to yet another.

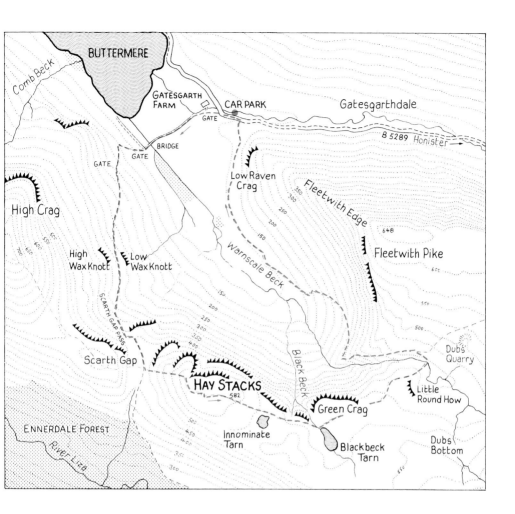

From here there is a good view west to Ennerdale. Even before the Forestry Commission planted the valley it was rather dour, though in medieval times this country was well-wooded and was called Ennerdale Chase, between the great deer preserves of Derwentfells and Copeland. On the southern shore of Ennerdale Water is a small deciduous wood once famous for its red deer, and it is recorded that as late as 1675 it contained 'Hartts and Staggs as great as in any part of England'. So this was a favoured area, perhaps following a tradition dating back thousands of years, for the dale is littered with enigmatic fragments of pre-history, culminating in the

mysterious cairn on Boat How above the wood already mentioned.

The fells towards Ennerdale Water are less rugged than those close to Buttermere because the rock is igneous, an intrusion of pink granophyre which weathers quicker than the blue-green Borrowdale Volcanic Series. Further away to the west of Ennerdale Water the geology changes again, to the heavily weathered Skiddaw Slate.

Go to the left of a small shallow tarn, then left of another iron post and up to the summit of Hay Stacks.

79

In fact the summit takes the form of a ridge, 50m long, with posts at its north and south pinnacles. This is very convenient in that it is possible to concentrate first on the north view without being too distracted with what is over your shoulder. The northern panorama also has the advantage of catching the best of the light, offering a magnificent sweep from High Crag in the foreground, across Crummock Water to Whiteless Pike, then Crag Hill, Robinson, Causey Pike (in the distance), Hindsgarth and Fleetwith Pike.

Having spent a few minutes on the northern pinnacle of the ridge (in fact this is probably the higher of the two at about 582m (1,909ft)), pick your way over the rocks to the south post. The north side of Great Gable and its neighbours is usually in deep shadow and this flattens the perspective. They menace and threaten rather than invite the walker; Scafell Pike, to the right of Gable, has an undeniable attraction however, being the highest peak in England. Of the other goliaths Pillar, to the south-west, rivals Great Gable in its presence and power. The north face of Pillar Rock is visible, which earned the rounded mountain its name and makes it a favourite with climbers.

From the summit scramble down to the cairned path which makes its way south-east close to the northern edge of the mountain block. Take care not to stray from the path. Make for the left of the tarn.

This is Innominate Tarn, which seems a silly name considering it was once known as Loaf Tarn. Presumably when the little loaf-shaped islands eroded and sank that name was considered inappropriate, since when it has remained innominate, i.e. un-named.

Most of the tarns in the area are very poor in aquatic plants because their water is drawn from thin peat overlying hard vol-canic rocks, which will not weather to release any minerals or nutrients. The Borrowdale Volcanics originated about 450 million years ago as a series of volcanic islands, their lavas, dust and debris of a similar type to those found in the Andes today. The precise date for any igneous rock is difficult to judge because there are no fossils to provide comparative clues.

Descend through a gap, passing to the right of a rocky outcrop, and down the cairned path.

A fine vista of Buttermere and Crummock Water suddenly opens on the left, framed by a cleft in the rock wall through which Black Beck runs. Blackbeck Tarn, which appears after a few more metres of walking, is a much prettier piece of water than the others encountered, edged by a moss carpet and with an obvious catchment and outfall.

Cross the stream just to the left of the tarn, then head north-east with Green Crag to the left and a wide marshy basin to the right.

View from Hay Stacks summit — north-west clockwise to south-east

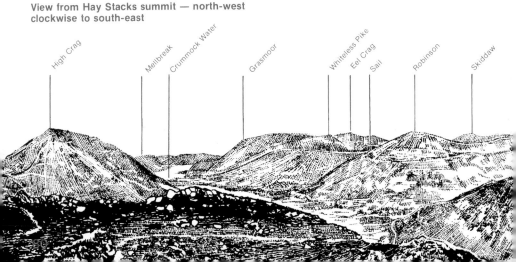

High Crag   Mellbreak   Crummock Water   Grasmoor   Whiteless Pike   Eel Crag   Sail   Robinson   Skiddaw

Innominate Tarn, Great Gable dominating the distant view

The bogs and puddles to the right resemble a tundra landscape, dominated by heather and *Sphagnum* moss. Squeeze the moss and you will see why it is so popular with gardeners making hanging baskets; it retains water. A similar property for centuries earned it a role in war-time as a combat-dressing, absorbing blood. One of the most interesting characteristics of *Sphagnum*, however, is that it is the prime constituent of peat, and its raw undecayed remains often go down more than a metre, the waterlogged conditions preserving both the moss and other plant remains like pollen grains. These tell scientists what the vegetation was like thousands of years ago.

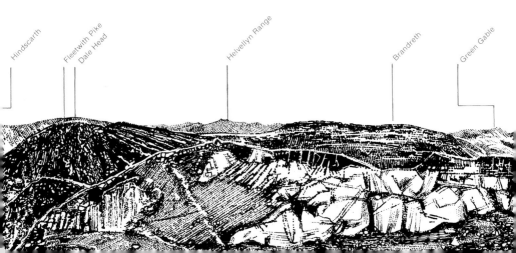

Hindscarth   Fleetwith Pike   Dale Head   Helvellyn Range   Brandreth   Green Gable

The path bears left of the rock outcrop of Little Round How, then descends a little to cross Warnscale Beck.

To the right is Dubs Bottom, the wide basin collecting run-off water from Grey Knotts and Brandreth which finds its way to Buttermere via Warnscale Beck. Ahead is the relic of Dubs Quarry, an eyesore of blue slate spoil.

Bear left along a narrow path through heather, joining a track after about 200m. Continue left.

The track is an old quarry road which winds tortuously down to Gatesgarth. Warnscale Beck to the left has attractive cascades and waterfalls, flanked by rocky promontories which provide pleasant vantage points. Ahead on the left is the sinister north face of Hay Stacks.

Warnscale Bottom, with Buttermere and Crummock Water in the distance

The track turns sharp right, then bears left.

An impressive view, like looking from a balcony high up in the Albert Hall.

The scree slopes of Hay Stacks support few trees other than rowan, but the west face of Fleetwith Pike also has yew, holly and hawthorn. Further down the valley is a clump of mature Scots pine, planted for shelter.

After another sharp left turn the track bears right and descends more gradually.

The lower slopes to the right are covered with a dense canopy of bracken for much of the year, which eliminates most other plants. To the left is a good view of Buttermere Fell and the ascent route to Scarth Gap.

Continue along the track which bears left to meet the road. Turn left to the car park.

Walk Fourteen
RANNERDALE

BUTTERMERE VILLAGE — HAUSE POINT — RANNERDALE — GYLL WOOD; 6km

A very varied walk with excellent views of Crummock Water and Buttermere, a look at several inter-esting little woods, and a good stride up grassy paths and a hidden valley.

Park in Buttermere village. Start at GR 174169 facing the Fish Hotel, and walk right to a car park. Leave the car park at its far right corner (beware of chickens!) and follow the way-marked path towards Crummock Water, keeping to the left of the stream.

The old village of Buttermere once had a Scandinavian-style 'click mill' to grind oats and rye. This was situated several hundred metres upstream and predated the Victorian enlargement of the village for the tourist trade.

To the left across the flat pasture is Scales Wood, a fine oakwood very different in character to the larchwood of Burtness on the east side of Sourmilk Gill. Above Scales Wood runs an old enclosure wall, then there is a steep slope before a wide corrie created and fashioned by ice, called Ling Comb. 'Ling' is another name for heather, and even from this distance it is possible to make out a thick collar of the plant clothing the hillside beneath Lingcomb Edge.

Continue along the path for several hundred metres until a bridge crosses the stream.

The symmetrical mound of woodland on the shore of Crummock Water is called Nether How, whilst across the beck to the right is Long How. How (or 'Howe') means a burial mound, and these two small hills are said in the novel *The Secret Valley* to be the resting place for English soldiers following a battle against the Normans. The details are all fictitious of course, but perhaps both these hills were burial sites at one time.

Today they are heavily wooded and are rich in wildlife. There seems to be a constant two-way traffic of birds between the two sites; wood pigeons are the most numerous, but great-spotted woodpeckers and jays are also regular commuters. Jays, noisy birds, are most noticeable in the autumn when they are much less shy and are busy collecting acorns. It has been calculated that each jay picks up an average of 3,000 acorns a year, burying them in nooks and crannies for winter food. Not all the acorns are found again of course, and it is possible that these birds are prime agents in the spread of oakwoods, far more important than the more obvious squirrels.

The relationship between acorns and jays has been known for many years. Writing in the 18th century William Cowper observed (of an acorn)

Thou wast a bauble once: a cup and ball,
Which babes might play with, and the
thievish jay
Seeking her food, with ease might have
purloin'd
The auburn nut that held thee . . . . .

Turn right and cross the bridge, then turn right again and follow the beck back up-stream for about 75m.

The strange wooden structure across the beck is a watergate, a device to prevent sheep from creeping around the sides of the stone walls into greener pasture via the stony bed of the stream. Whatever the volume of water the hinged gate will act as a barrier without interrupting the flow.

The path divides; follow a rather steep path which bears left, away from the beck, and north-east through Long How.

The ground soon levels-off and the wide woodland path is very attractive. The oaks are at their most lovely in June when the leaves are still fresh and cock redstarts are searching among the mossy stumps for insects.

The path leads to a wicket gate and onto a main road. Turn left for about 100m then right (the line of the former road) and continue until it rejoins the metalled road again. Keep on the road around a double bend, then take a gently rising green path right, up the hillside.

bedding, so it is of little value to farmers. Neither is it a foodplant of many insects, only a sawfly, a few bugs and beetles, and a nondescript moth called the brown silver-lines, so it is of little interest to the naturalist.

Continue along the path for about 200m, at which point stop for a view over Crummock Water.

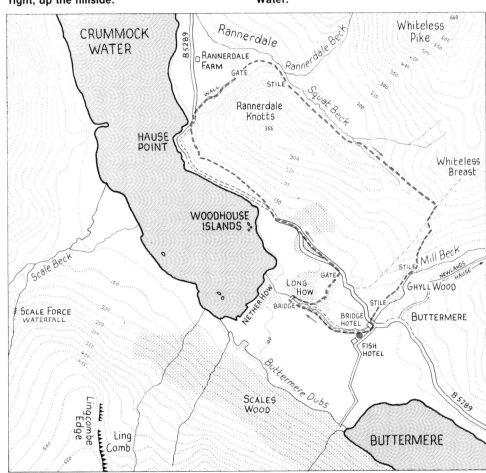

Bracken and gorse are usually taken as indicators that the soil is deep and of sufficient quality at least to grow a good grass crop. Fortunately for the visitor the Lakeland farmers are encouraged by grants and subsidies not to damage the visual beauty of the lower fells by 'improving' them. Bracken is poisonous to stock for most of the year and is no longer used for

The name is probably derived from 'Crombok-watre' i.e. crooked water, which is appropriate as the south quarter is distinctly kinked. There are several islands, all close to the shore and covered by birch and heather which provide shelter for visiting grey-lag and Canada geese. The cormorants are not so fussy and often sit exposed on the rocks of the Woodhouse

A Herdwick sheep on the slopes of Rannerdale Knotts

Islands to dry their wings.

Across the lake is an arc of flattish land marking the outfall of Scale Beck. This wide grassy area was once inhabited by an Iron Age or Romano-British tribe and several stone huts have been discovered, suggesting it was a favoured settlement. Scale Beck soon gains height, bearing to the left (south) where a furrow of trees screens the famous Scale Force, a 47m (156ft) cascade of water marking the geological boundary between the old, soft Skiddaw Slate and a harder intrusion of granophyre.

Ignore any paths to the right and continue up the main path to a rocky outcrop.

Herdwick sheep are usually to be seen around this spot, possibly enjoying the view. Their fleece was once used undyed to make a tweed called 'Hodden grey', but today the wool of most upland breeds is used for carpets. The view ahead from the brow of the hill is of the road flanked by Crummock Water to the left and the imposing bulk of Grasmoor to the right.

Descend steeply to join the road again. Turn right almost immediately and go up the track with the wall to your left.

The steep, lightly-wooded slopes of Rannerdale Knotts cast a heavy shadow over this section of the walk. The drystone wall encloses in-bye pasture towards Rannerdale Farm and was built from that side with the cam of capstones protruding this side. It takes two men a day to build about six metres of wall, and each half-metre of stones weighs about a tonne. Anything less than its present height and the wall would not be stockproof, for sheep are capable of amazingly silly vertical scrambles.

85

Despite its name this is a very attractive stream, ash-lined, with some unassuming little falls and a conversational babble. The lower slopes of Rannerdale Knotts, to the right, are littered with boulders which provide breeding sites for wheatears, one of the most attractive of the upland birds with a distinctive white rump. This identification feature earned the bird its name, but propriety corrupted the vernacular 'arse' to 'ear'.

The rock boulders from Rannerdale Knotts are paler than those from a kilometre to the south or north; recent geological investigation has suggested there was probably an intrusion or injection of molton rock beneath the surface which baked the local stone and gave it its distinctive khaki colour.

Walk along parallel with the stream to a ladder stile over a wall to the right. After crossing this continue south-east, still parallel with Squat Beck.

After a while the valley seems to open out, the stream falters, and Rannerdale takes on a silent aspect, as if waiting. Rannerdale was the site of a great 11th century battle between the English, under Earl Boethar, and the invading Normans, under Ranulf le Meschin, in which there was much bloodshed and the English for once were victorious. Historians will say that no such battle actually happened and that Nicholas Size invented it for his novel *The Secret*

Wheatear

Continue to a wicket gate, after which the path bears right.

Grasmoor to the north is still the major element in the landscape but closer at hand to the east is Whiteless Pike, a 654m (2,159ft) beauty which, from this angle at least, looks as though it has escaped from an alpine calendar. Separating the two mountains is Rannerdale Beck.

Follow the path right, past a tree, to join Squat Beck.

View from col at head of Rannerdale Valley — south-east clockwise to north-west

Snockrigg   Green Gable   Great Gable   Hay Stacks   Kirk Fell   High Crag   Buttermere   High Stile   Chapel Crags   Dodd   Red Pike

Squat Beck in November

Valley, but there is no doubt that for some reason the Normans failed to penetrate into the northern Lake District, and the Domesday Book is strangely silent about the area. So perhaps Norman ghosts linger on the hillsides to right and left, lamenting their defeat.

Continue up the dale, keeping to the path.

Minor detours may be necessary around marshy dips and hollows; the worst ones are covered with bog moss which is usually bright green and therefore easy to avoid. There are dozens of different kinds of bog moss, all very beautiful if you have boots and can peer closely at them. Botanists like David Bellamy may slosh around with reckless zeal but such commitment is unnecessary; look for the beautiful red-flushed species called *Sphagnum rubellum,* growing on the drier hummocks, among the more usual *Sphagnum plumulosum.* To the left several small streams run diagonally to meet Squat Beck, their deeply furrowed courses cutting through Skiddaw Slate.

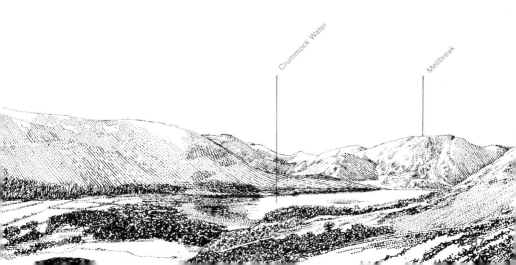

Crummock Water

Mellbreak

Look back down the valley for a distant view of Loweswater.

The crest is reached quite suddenly between rocky outcrops to either side.

The block of hillside immediately ahead is High Snockrigg, with Robinson (736m) a little to the left. Further to the right, beyond Buttermere and Warnscale Bottom, are the craggy peaks of Hay Stacks with Great Gable behind and to the left. The route up Hay Stacks via Scarth Gap, described in walk 13, can be seen towards High Crag.

Turn right, down a broad grassy track for about 100m, then take a left turn where the paths divide and descend the steep path in the direction of Buttermere village.

To the left is the Mill Beck and the road to Newlands Hause. Whiteless Breast is on the north side of this, with Knott Rigg in the distance.

Turning back to the south-west, across the Buttermere—Crummock Water valley is

Lingcomb Edge again. This time look to the left, to the peaks of Red Pike and High Stile.

High Stile and its associates to the south-east are composed of hard volcanic rocks called the Borrowdale Volcanic Series or Greenstone, whilst most of Red Pike consists of an intrusion called Ennerdale Granophyre capped by a baked layer of Skiddaw Slate which has given the peak a smoother silhouette.

Continue the descent diagonally left until a path leads off left again, down to the edge of a valley wood. Make for a gated stile, go over this and turn right. Continue parallel with the Mill Beck.

This is Gyll Wood, a very steep 'hanging' sessile oakwood once used as a coppice and now owned by the National Trust. To the left is Mill Beck, making its way through an attractive little gully down to the Bridge Hotel.

Go through the stile, left at the road then right to get back to the Fish Hotel.

Crummock Water from the south-east, above Buttermere village

'Whin' means gorse, so it can be assumed that when the first Norse-Irish settlers arrived they found the slopes heavily clad with the plant and used it for kindling and grazing.

Walk Fifteen
BRACKENTHWAITE

LANTHWAITE — BRACKENTHWAITE HOWS — CRUMMOCK WATER; 5km

Brackenthwaite Hows stands at the strategic meeting place between the north-west fells and the green corridor of Lorton Vale. The river Cocker meets the Derwent just outside the National Park boundary at Cockermouth, 11km to the north, but long before then the hills have lost their grandeur and the lattice of fields has become the controlling influence on the landscape. This walk embraces a view of the vale from the foot of Grasmoor and Whiteside, then crosses farmland and common to Lanthwaite Wood and the shores of Crummock Water; there are several moderate inclines but nothing too severe – an appropriate finale with some abiding impressions of northern Lakeland.

Start at the Lanthwaite car park, GR 158207. Walk north past the farm then bear right along a track through open fell.

The view is totally dominated by Grasmoor to the right, an awesome 846m (2,791ft) peak which from this angle looks impossibly steep. In fact there is a straightforward walking route from the other side which can be reached by following Liza Beck to the head of Gasgale Gill and up onto a grassy plateau, but this still involves more than 600m of ascent. To the left is Whiteside, 702m (2,317ft), but of less dramatic aspect. Whin Ben on its southern flank is,

After a few hundred metres a track junction is reached. Bear right, to reach Liza Beck.

The fan-shaped weir is edged by rushes, identified by their round, spiky leaves. Soft round rushes were once harvested and used as a crude form of domestic lighting. The tough husks were stripped away to reveal wads of white spongy pith which were dipped in sheep fat and used as primitive candles, called rush lights.

Bear right, heading upstream for about 100m, cross the footbridge and follow the path uphill. After a few metres the path divides; take the left fork and head north, keeping close to the wall.

In the distance to the left (west) is Holme Wood, a large block of mixed conifers with some curiously-shaped plantings of larch. Loweswater lies at its foot but is totally obscured by a wide dome of farmland and Brackenthwaite Hows. The hamlet of Loweswater (just visible) was once an important little settlement, and by the 12th century it had its own chapel. It did not have a burying ground however, and corpses had to be transported to St Bees, more than 20km to the south-west. They were 'buried in woollens' first (one of many legal stipulations brought in to protect the woollen industry), then strapped to a horse and carried up the hillside to a first stopping point at the boulders beyond Holme Force ('Grey Mare's Tail'), from thence across Burnbank Fell and to the Cumbrian coast.

Continue for several hundred metres, with the wall to your left.

To the right are the frost-shattered screes of Whiteside End. The rock is Skiddaw Slate, a 500 million-year-old bed of shale laced with hard sandstone slabs and more recent bands of quartz. To avoid the current confusion implied by its title geologists have recently taken to calling the rock the 'Skiddaw Series', a much better name for such a varied assortment.

The pasture to the left is grazed by a herd of Highland cattle, kept for beef, though the need for hardy stock has been superseded with the introduction of wintering sheds. The longhorn ancestors of the Highland breed were brought into Britain from south-west Europe by Neolithic settlers, and probably graced Lorton Vale several thousand years ago.

The extensive walling of lower fells for fields or 'intak' was a phenomenon of the 18th and 19th centuries, particularly following enclosure awards by the government, but the history of walling goes back longer than this and there were many periods of enclosure, usually dictated by necessity, as, for example, when groups of medieval farmers tried to grow corn in the valleys and needed to exclude stock.

Look for a wicket gate through the wall to the left. Go through this and follow the wall, ahead then right, then straight down to a stile by the Liza Beck. Cross this at a footbridge, then turn left down the road.

Skylark nest

Take care on the road; cars are moving quickly on this section of the B 5289. The wall on the right is set into the bank, enabling plants like polypod and parsley fern to thrive, whilst the verge in summer contains wood sage and red campion.

Just after Beck House is a gate on the right waymarked 'path to Scale Hill'. Go through this and west, past Pickett Howe.

The rocky knoll to the left (south) marks the edge of a mixed plantation, dominated here by oak. To the north is an interesting farmstead, the farmhouse to the right and a fine 'bank barn' in the centre, its imposing rear doorway built to accommodate loaded carts. To the left are some low outbuildings, possibly built as a kennel or pig sty, then on the far left a new shed and silage clamp.

Proceed along the wall for about 300m then, when the wall veers right, continue uphill straight ahead over tussocky grass-land and heath, making for a solitary rowan tree with a mixed fir plantation on the hillcrest beyond.

The route is very indistinct but keep heading south, uphill towards the fir trees.

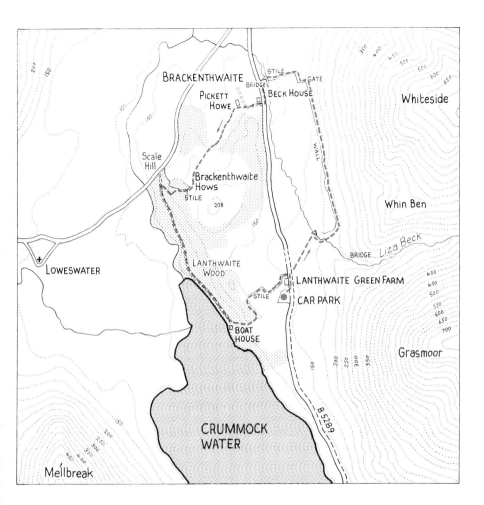

The ground is marshy at first but the tussocky grassland soon dries out and the land is in fact very old pasture, excellent for wild flowers and nesting birds like the skylark. For several centuries lark's tongue in aspic was a popular delicacy, as was lark pie. 'If the number of individuals sacrificed to the exigencies of the kitchen can be trusted to supply a criterion, the skylark has long been a very abundant bird in Lakeland' was the observation of H. A. Macpherson in 1892, a wry if guarded criticism of the traditional slaughter. Today skylarks are the most widespread of all our breeding birds, restricted in some areas by changes in agriculture but still abundant.

Past the rowan tree continue in the same line. There is an indistinct path which improves further up the hill. Make for the wood, with a stone wall ahead and to the right.

Just before the wall is a very hummocky area; look closely and most of the hummocks will be found to bear clusters of rabbit droppings. Far from wishing to conceal their daily functions many animals actually use them to mark their territories on the most exposed vantage points they can find. Because rabbits are herbivores they produce vast quantities of fibrous pellets which build and fertilise the hummocks. Carnivorous animals do the same sort of thing but not in such profusion.

Naturalists learn a great deal about the habits and food of wild animals by looking for their droppings, though to an untrained eye one stool can look much like another. The scent is the vital factor however, and even to unsophisticated nostrils an otter 'spraint' smells not unpleasantly of fish-oil and musk whilst the rather similar-looking mink dropping produces an unutterably evil stench. So if you see someone on his hands and knees sniffing a rather questionable substance, there is a chance he might be involved in a scientific investigation.

Rabbit

Rabbits are not as common as they used to be. They were introduced into this country as a source of food, probably by the Normans, and have a long history of exploitation in carefully controlled warrens; but the population suddenly escalated to about 100 million in the early part of this century, and myxomatosis was introduced from the continent in the 1950s to control the numbers. It did this spectacularly, and fresh outbreaks of the horrific disease still keep the population in check, to the relief of most farmers.

Follow the wall as it climbs uphill, narrowing with a rock outcrop on the left. On the near skyline is a larch tree; take the indistinct path up the slope to this, then turn right and walk about 30m to a stile through the wall. This leads into a wood; continue along the path with a wall to your right.

This is the northern border of Lanthwaite Wood, once composed of sessile oak but now an eccentric assortment; even so there are enough oaks to attract a few of the characteristic birds like pied flycatcher and redstart. There are several Scots pines to the left, not the normal tall types associated with plantations but low-crowned trees with buttressed trunks, more like the genuine natives of the Scottish Highlands.

After about 150m the path turns sharp left, then zig-zags down via a series of steps to join a track.

This is a very attractive section of the walk, common heather and bell heather lining the craggy slopes and the tree canopy breaking every now and then to reveal Crummock Water and the hamlet of Loweswater.

Turn left along the track.

The vegetation is remarkably luxuriant, not because the soil is especially good but because sheep are excluded. Ungrazed, the floors of most Lake District woods would be like this, supporting a thick quilt of bilberry, heather and woodrush.

To the right, screened by the trees, is the river Cocker. Its name is derived from the old British 'cucra', meaning crooked stream.

Ignore any side-tracks and continue to descend, to the lake shore.

A classic view of Crummock Water suddenly opens out, framed by tall pines; looking south over the lake Mellbreak is to the right and Rannerdale Knotts to the left, with Red Pike and High Stile in the distance. The glacier that shaped the valley flowed from that direction, chiselling a wide corridor that eventually acted as a trough for its own meltwater. Crummock Water is clean and deep, and, like Ennerdale Water and Wastwater, a large part of its yield is drawn-off unadulterated and pumped south to slake the thirst of industrial Lancashire. Its shores are barren because aquatic or marginal plants find the substrate too poor in mineral nutrients, and the narrow band of shoreline pebbles shelves suddenly, sometimes precipitously, to a maximum depth of 44m (144ft). Crummock Water is a beautiful, austere lake that is not so confined or compromised as its sister to the south.

Boathouse on the north-east shore of Crummock Water

Bear left along a path leading to a wide stony track with the lake to your right. Go along this until just before a boathouse, then take the path which bears left up through the wood. This bears round to the left and eventually joins a grassy track. Turn right along this, leading out of the wood.

Suddenly Grasmoor is once again the centrepiece, impossible to ignore.

The wall to the left has a distinct gap in it, from the footing to about half way up. With such an unyielding medium, the skilled wallers who made and maintained these field boundaries displayed great skill and

View from northern end of Crummock Water — south-east clockwise to south-west

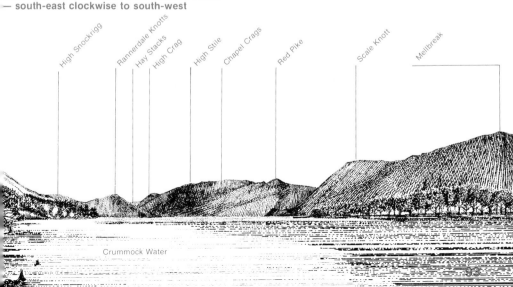

High Snockrigg | Rannerdale Knotts | Hay Stacks | High Crag | High Stile | Chapel Crags | Red Pike | Scale Knott | Mellbreak

Crummock Water

imagination in accommodating the require-ments of farmers and landowners. Many of the gaps were constructed to allow runnels or streams to flow unhindered, but others were put there to let animals move freely between fields. 'Hogg-holes' allowed young sheep to reach better pasture, 'smoots' enticed rabbits to walk into hinged traps.

Walk across the field keeping to the right of the wall and go over a stile, then bear right and left towards Lanthwaite Green Farm.

Another excellent example of a very old farm, its origins lost in the period up to the 17th century when yeoman farmers or 'statesmen' were living through a comfortable page of history, their prosperity underpinned by the value of wool. Just over the page in the 18th century lurked disaster, bad winters, wars and inflation, but by then many of the yeoman families had turned aristocrat and the farms were left to a poorer breed whose main object was to stay alive. Thus the body of this farm, greatly altered, remained functional and is still a working unit today, but the soul lies hidden in the modest core of old stonework.

Go to the left around the farm, then turn right along the road and back to the car park.

Raven

◁ *Highland cattle, dwarfed by Whiteside End*

*If you have enjoyed these walks don't hang up
your boots: other WALKS TO REMEMBER will
be available soon!*

Published by
Polecat Press Ltd
Registered Office
63 High Bridge
Newcastle Upon Tyne
NE1 1DU